# A Cup of Roses

## Stories by 8 Writers

Gold-Kroll Publishing

# A Cup of Roses

## Stories by 8 Writers

Ruth Frankel–Graner

Gerda Frieberg

Carol Green

Sam Hoffer

Raizie Jacobson

Fiona Gold Kroll

David Rapoport

Jenny Roger

Published by Gold-Kroll Publishing
www.fionagoldkroll.com



EDITOR: Fiona Gold Kroll
COPY EDITOR: Robert Kroll
ORIGINAL COVER ARTWORK: Ruth Frankel-Graner
COVER AND INTERIOR DESIGN: Daniella Postavsky

ISBN 978-0-9952847-1-5(Paperback)
ISBN 978-0-99528747-2-2 (EPUB)
ISBN 978-0-9952847-0-8 (KINDLE)

This is an original print edition of *A Cup of Roses, Stories by 8 Writers*.

*To Ruth*

# Table of contents

# Introduction

Throughout human history, stories have been the most effective method for conveying meaning, information, and lessons. Judaism, both as a religious tradition and a cultural civilization, has relied upon storytelling to pass on teachings from generation to generation. In the Talmudic era, it is even told that students would leave the lecture-room of Rabbi Chiyya, who was known for legal exposition. They would flock, instead, to Rabbi Abbahu, the storyteller (B. Sotah 40a). No matter the brilliance of a legal exposition, stories add a layer of soulfulness, of relatability, that touches the heart of every person.

In truth, storytelling is nothing less than art, perhaps the oldest art-form of human history. Like in a painting, we travel through brush-strokes of experience, action, and reflection. In a great work of art, you can always find a story.

In that tradition, the contributors to this volume have done much more than produce entertainment. They have taken very personal reflections, intimate experiences, and unique insights, and turned them into art. This takes courage and a true willingness to grow. They are to be congratulated for this magnificent compilation.

Personal growth defines the life of Ruth Frankel-Graner, of blessed memory, who inspired this book. I was privileged to know her and work with her through Beth Tikvah. She is one of the finest people I have ever met in my life. Ruth was a teacher who derived personal satisfaction by watching her students achieve. She saw the power of art to inspire self-confidence and heal the broken experiences of the past.

Students, young and old, remember Ruth as someone who devoted her life to helping others. She inspired this book not only by encouraging its publication, but by motivating each participant to grow personally through the art of storytelling.

Today, communication is prized for being quick, witty, and to-the-point. While that may be effective, it is not art. In this volume, the authors invite you to join them on adventures. They want you to discover what they discovered. They want you to feel, to believe, and engage. Most importantly, they want you to enjoy. Not because these tales will give you a quick laugh. But because they are beautiful. Plain and simple – just beautiful.

*Rabbi Jarrod Grover – Senior Spiritual Leader*
*Beth Tikvah Synagogue*
*Toronto*

# Preface

In the fall of 2012, Ruth Frankel-Graner began a creative writers' group at Beth Tikvah Synagogue in Toronto. Ruth was an accomplished writer and artist; a graduate of the University of Toronto (Art and Archaeology, English Literature), and York University (Fine Arts). She was a Specialist Teacher of English, Special Education and Art. Several of her writings were published in literary journals, magazines and newspapers. A short story (non- fiction) "Candace," was a second prize winner in a Canadian Woman Studies Journal contest, and a painting of the birth of her son Paul "The Night You Were Born Paul Darling," won an award in a Royal Bank of Canada competition. In addition to all her accomplishments, she was a devoted mother and grandmother.

Ruth often mused that the group should write and publish an Anthology of short stories. Somehow they never got around to it. Occasionally, the group met at her home, and after receiving a bouquet of roses from one member, Ruth sent a hand painted thank you note with a picture of a cup and huge red rose on the front with a message of friendship.

Ruth passed away suddenly in October 2015. Shocked and saddened, the writers' group took several weeks to meet again, but they knew Ruth would have wanted them to stay together. And, they did. When the idea of an Anthology was tossed around, everyone unanimously agreed to contribute their work. A Cup of Roses was a meaningful choice for the cover and the title of the book.

Each petal representing stories by 8 writers. *A Cup of Roses, Stories by 8 Writers* is Ruth's legacy.

*Fiona Gold Kroll, Toronto*

# Heading South? Eater Beware: or How I Saved an Entire Country from Disaster

*Ruth Frankel-Graner*

A few notes of salsa or merengue, the scent of guaria morada, and a long buried memory comes bubbling to the surface of my febrile, conscious mind. Or maybe it's an e-mail from a friend who was grilled by customs officials about the contents of the lunch she planned to eat on a flight to a warmer climate. That's when I remembered: Single-handedly, I had saved an entire country from disaster. Admittedly, it was a rather small country—Costa Rica but it was a very large disaster—potentially. And like Eve's cataclysmic impulse, it all began with an apple.

Many, many years ago, I took an apple to Costa Rica. I hadn't intended to. I took it as part of my lunch, even told the customs official who asked "Bringing any food?"

"Yes," I replied in all honesty, "I have my lunch to eat on the plane." He didn't ask what was in that lunch. (Times change.) But surprisingly, the miniature lunch served on the plane was not only identifiable, it was also quite tasty, and since I ate it along with the supersized chocolate bar I had in my purse, I had no need for my designer apple at that point – it was organic and worth about $3.37 – so I stowed it in my capacious carry-on bag.

Arriving at our luxurious, albeit gated hotel, too early to get into our room, while others of a less cerebral nature dashed for the ocean and its coarser delights, my brainy friend and I headed for a tour of a botanical garden. That was when (as the evidence will show,) I transferred the aforesaid apple to my smaller purse. Who knew? I might get hungry. And I did.

We stood in line and bought tickets at the fabled botanical garden, and stood in line waiting for a guide to lead us through it. That was when the crime of gastronomic passion occurred. I ate the apple. Being both botanically and hygienically oriented, I threw my apple core into a large garbage bin, one might even say a huge garbage bin, but not before wrapping it up in one of those nifty full-sized white paper towels you can pinch from those pint-sized airplane washrooms. It was relatively early in the botanical garden's garbage day, and so the apple core landed in a garbage bin which was almost empty. It touched down with a soft, even dainty clunk. I envisioned it as eventually disappearing harmlessly into the maelstrom of island refuse. How wrong I was!

The tour began. We ambled past the very sensual Chelone lyonii, ("Hot Lips" to those in the know) oohed at the very poisonous Brugmansia sanguinea, and ahhed at the very orange Clivia mineata. At about this point our guide began to talk about the fragility of the Costa Rican ecological system, the dangers of importing even a single new vegetal element into this island country.

This could apply to any country! Hadn't I spent many summers at the cottage vacuuming truckloads of loathsome ladybugs, imported to Canada to finish off some other loathsome bugs—aphids? Hasn't the purple loosestrife, an illegal immigrant, been the source of too much strife? (Talk about the man who came to dinner!) – along with the ear-splitting nail-on blackboard-scraping-endless hours of starling jabber, from unlovable birds who arrived in Canada because our neighbours to the south –well one in particular –believed that all birds mentioned in the work of William Shakespeare deserved a roost in the U.S. (I'm not making this up!) But these were for the most part, unintentional betrayals of our ecology.

Was I about to inflict knowingly the same on Costa Rica? As my young friend Paige would say, "Not on my pie-crust!" (Apple pie I'm sure.)

I had to get that apple core back, and quickly. But there was a problem with leaving the group and heading back on my own to the garbage bin. It's called a sense of direction. I wasn't even in a familiar hemisphere. How far would I stray? My husband often said I was the only woman he knew who walked out of her house and couldn't find the garage— which was attached. But despite my tropical surroundings, and the scary-sounding "rain forest," I had a conscience, there was a path, and it seemed fairly straight. I hurried all the way back to the garbage bin. I wondered if it would be overflowing with refuse. How deep was I willing to troll? Very!

But the gods of ecology were smiling that day. Only a thin layer of junk concealed my paper-wrapped apple core. I counted to three, held my breath and dove in. Gotcha! There were no witnesses, since everybody waiting in the new line was staring at Pachira Aquatica hoping, I guess, to get rich quick. (It's common name is The Money Tree.) Deftly, I popped the apple core into my purse. Back at the hotel, I put it in my suitcase, but not before wrapping it in the plastic bag which held my soap. The soap would have to fend for itself. And then I forgot all about it!

That means I passed back through customs and the form which probably asked was I bringing in any plant material. Of course in a way, I wasn't. I was returning some plant material. But as I say, I had forgotten anyhow. Until I arrived home and unpacked. There it was, rust-coloured and wrinkled. Rigor mortis had definitely set in. I disposed of the apple corpse, urr apple core, without a trace in the usual manner: garbage chute since my condo does not compost, as yet.

Until this confession, no one has known of my selfless deed. Yes, I single-handedly saved Costa Rica from ecological disaster, and finally, since it happened in another century, I feel it is safe to say so. No medals, ribbons or parades, please. I am content in the knowledge that ignorance is not always bliss.

# Broken Dreams

*Gerda Frieberg*

WWII ended on May 8, 1945, the same day I was liberated from the concentration camp by the Soviet Army. My mother and sister Hana survived. We crisscrossed Europe in search of any relatives. Sadly, we found none. We were stateless refugees stuck on the blood soaked soil of Germany. The American Army set up refugee camps in the obsolete German army bases. After a long journey we arrived at the displaced persons camp in Landsberg am Lech, Bavaria. It was erev Yom Kippur. American soldiers were posted at the entrance gate. There was no need for permission to leave the camp. I just was not sure whether the soldiers were protecting the survivors, or the German population, in case our boys would take revenge. They did not realize that Holocaust Survivors did not stoop to that level.

The United Nations Relief Agency provided food and clothing, which was collected in the U.S.A. Food and clothing were not the only things we needed. We also needed money, whether to pay for a bus ride into town, buy soap, shampoo, any medication, or see a dentist after so many years of neglect.

When we arrived, the camp had already housed six-thousand Survivors, who had organized a committee and elected a president to become our spokesman. In order to secure the needs of the community, one of the buildings was set up as a hospital, in which surviving doctors and nurses were on call. Another building was set up as a school for children, who survived in the Soviet Union, in Convents, or with the partisans in the forests. One building housed teenage orphans, who called the place their kibbutz. Outside the gate of the camp, a house was used for daily prayers and Holiday services.

Remembering my father's last words, while being taken away by the Nazi's "Take care of mother till I return," it now became my responsibility to take the first step into a new chapter in my life. Survivors were offered free tuition at universities. It would have been a dream come true to finish my education, which was denied to Jewish students under the Nazi regime. But at this point my priority was to earn some money.

My memory drifted back to 1939. I was 13 years old when the war started, I was no longer allowed to go to school. I was devastated. My mother sent me to a seamstress, just to keep me occupied. Home economics, which was an obligatory subject was not my priority in school. Maria taught me how to use the sewing machine. I had a chance to watch her cut fabric that her clients brought, and then create a garment. Unfortunately, six weeks later, my sewing lessons came to an end, when all Jews of Upper Silesia were deported to a ghetto in Poland. Overnight we became homeless and poor. We did not imagine what lay ahead of us.

After years of indescribable hardship, we finally found a temporary home in the DP camp.

But how does one begin to rebuild a life? We had only one room with two beds, three chairs, a small table and a hot plate. I was able to squeeze a borrowed old sewing machine between the beds and someone found me an electric iron. Word got out that there was a seamstress in the building. The girls picked up the clothes that arrived in the camp, but most items needed some alteration. There was no shortage of customers. As time went by, I gradually progressed to dressmaking.

My sister Hana met her beloved in camp, and got married. Soon they decided to go to what was then Palestine. By that time, I had earned enough money to explore the state of Bavaria with Mother. We traveled to the mountains, lakes, royal castles and museums, and purchased tickets to the opera and theater performances.

The DP camp was supposed to be our temporary home. But where could we go? No country opened the doors for us. With the help of the Red Cross, some survivors found relatives who had left Europe before the war. Residents of the United States, Canada and Australia were able to sponsor family members. But, we had no relatives in any of these countries.

Three years later, in 1948, we witnessed the birth of the State of Israel. The camp population was shrinking. Mother and I had no place to go. I still had enough customers to keep me busy. On Friday afternoon I would cover the sewing machine. I deserved a day of rest.

The camp was located near a river on the edge of the forest, and during the summer we spent most Saturdays there. One beautiful day, Mother and I decided to pack a picnic lunch, and go swimming in the river. Nearby I noticed some raspberry bushes. I thought why not get some berries for dessert? While picking berries, suddenly the head of a young man popped up on the other side of the bush. He introduced himself. We started a conversation.

"My name is Srulek, I come from Poland. I lost my entire family, except one brother," he said.

I invited him to have lunch with us. After lunch we just jumped into the river for a swim. The sun began to set; we went back to camp.

A few days later I heard a knock at the door, it was Srulek. "How did you find me?" I asked.

"You told me you are a dressmaker. I asked around, there was no problem, most people know you."

I was astonished. I had no expectation to meet anyone. My mother was my constant companion. Who is this young man who would take the trouble to find me? He told me he was living in the camp hospital and worked there in the kitchen as a chef. My first thought was, this is great! We had constant power failures in the camp and I would often sew by candle light, to finish any work I needed to complete by hand. I knew there was always power in the hospital.

"Would it be OK with you if I come to your place when the power is out?" I asked.

"No problem, I'll get a key, you can come any time, even when I am not there, because sometimes I work late."

I was so happy that I no longer had to work by candlelight to finish a dress on time as promised.

As I worked, the nurses came in and asked for Srulek. Lucky guy, I thought, he does not have to chase the girls, they chase after him. Then one day he asked me;

"Why do you work late into the evening?"

"There is nothing else to do," I answered.

"Maybe you would like to go to a movie?" he asked.

"That would be nice, but if you don't mind my mother will come with us."

"Not a problem," he said.

We received great news from the Red Cross. Mother's sister and her husband survived and were living in Switzerland.

They were our only living relatives. We found their address, and I decided to visit them. As refugees, we did not have any identification or passports. I took the train to the Swiss border, and in the middle of the night I slipped across. What a reunion. I had not seen my aunt and uncle since 1936. After all the hugs and kisses, my aunt told me she was so glad I had come.

"I am scheduled for surgery in Zurich, and while I am away you can look after your uncle," she said.

I had not planned to stay; I was there illegally.

There was no telephone in the D.P. Camp and I could only communicate with Mother by mail. I wrote and told her that I needed to stay and look after my uncle until after my aunt's surgery. Srulek in the meantime was in touch with Mother to find out when I would be back. After my aunt came home, she asked me to stay a bit longer to shop and help around the house. One day I walked in with groceries. My aunt opened the door, holding a letter in her hand.

"You can pack your bag and leave," she said.

I was puzzled and then she handed me a letter addressed to me. "Why did you open it?" I said.

"Your boyfriend wants you back."

Curious as to what made my aunt so angry, I read the letter.

Srulek wrote, "I thought you went for a vacation. If you wanted to work, you could have stayed here," was his first sentence.

I returned to the DP camp, happy to see Srulek and Mother. In the meantime, Srulek's brother left with his wife for Australia. By then we were no longer just friends. We fell in love.

Finally, he too had an opportunity to leave the D.P camp. His brother offered to send him a visa. One day while we took our evening stroll, he asked me what my plans were for the future.

"I have no idea. "Hana is in Israel, and Mother and I have nowhere to go." Srulek paused and took my hand.

"Will you marry me? As my wife you will be able to get a visa to Australia."

This was not a dream come true, it was a nightmare. Leaving mother was not an option. I had to make a decision. To follow the man I love would mean I would have to leave my mother behind. My father's plea to take care of Mother was embedded in my brain. Srulek left with the promise he would send a visa for Mother and me.

Time went by and the camp population was shrinking. I heard nothing from Srulek and Mother and I decided to go to Israel.

One day while walking in Tel Aviv, I met a girl I had not seen since she left the DP camp. "I live in Melbourne and just came to visit my Israeli family," she said.

"I met Srulek before I left; he lives nearby. He told me that he wrote to you, but all the letters were returned. He applied for a visa for you and your mother, and now he doesn't know where to find you. He wrote to your aunt, asking for your address, but she did not reply. I will tell him that I found you!" she said.

It was too late; I had just married three weeks earlier.

We lived in Israel for three years. The constant fear of war and conflict was not what I envisioned in my future. We chose Canada as a home for us and our children. My husband's brother also left Israel and joined his wife's relatives in Melbourne.

Thirty years passed and we received an invitation to their son's wedding. We were not going to miss the first wedding in the family, and decided to embark on this long journey. After the wedding, on the evening before our departure, a neighbour of my brother-in-law invited the whole family to their home.

As I entered the living room, I saw a gentleman standing near the fireplace. He looked at me, his face turned white like the ceiling. With trembling fingers, he reached into his jacket pocket, removed a photo and walked across the room towards me.

"Thirty years I carried your photo," he said. He turned to my husband.

"You are the luckiest man in the world."

He told me, that he was able to get a visa for me and my mother, but his letters to the camp were returned. He then wrote to my aunt and asked for my address. She did not reply.

"Come, I'll show you my home, I live just next door," he said. We entered the living room; he pointed to a violin on a side table.

"This kept me going, I was so lonely here, I thought of the time we spent in the DP camp. You introduced me to classical music. When I arrived in Australia I took violin lessons, and to this day whenever I pick up the violin I think of you."

Two years later I visited Melbourne again. This time for the wedding of my only relative whom I found after 30 years. By now my marriage had come to an end. Srulek found out that I was in town, and arrived at my cousin's home with a bouquet of roses.

We went for a walk in the park.

"I will leave my wife," he said. "Will you marry me?"

I was taken aback. With tears in my eyes, I replied.

"I could never build my happiness on someone's pain. We just have to accept that it was not destined for us to be together."

We stayed in touch by mail. On my next trip to Melbourne I found out that Srulek had been seriously injured in a car accident. He did not want me to see him. When I did not receive a card for Rosh Hashanah I realized that he was gone.

At the age of thirteen, my father asked me to take care of mother, and I did.

# How I Became a Jewish Writer

*Carol Green*

I am a Christian and I celebrate Christmas. I am also a Jewish writer and I celebrate Chanukah.  Let me explain.

When I was a young girl, I had a friend named Robyn who was Jewish. I really wanted to go to a Jewish summer camp with her. My Mother said they wouldn't let me go because I wasn't Jewish. You know what? She was right. Robyn wrote me letters from camp all summer about Nate and Josh and other boys she had crushes on. And I wasn't there.

In high school, I had a number of girlfriends who were Jewish. I sometimes took the Jewish holidays and got away with it. With a name like Green, it wasn't difficult.

On one of the holidays, I was at Robyn's house. Her Mom insisted on spoon-feeding me chopped liver. How could I refuse? Lucky for me, I love chopped liver. Hers was very good. Mrs. L.'s other claim to fame was that her maiden name was Cohen and she had a cousin named Lenny who worked in Montréal as a singer. Still does. You may be familiar with his work.

When I moved to upper school, I was a fixture at my friends Marilyn's and Marsha's households. I would go to Marilyn's house after school and we would hang out, listening to music. The Doors were big then.

Marsha's Dad was in the clothing business in Ottawa, and Marsha was well-dressed. She helped me to select outfits that were "classic." I recall listening to her younger brother, Stanley practice chanting for weeks before his Bar Mitzvah.

I don't know what became of Marsha, or Marilyn, as I lost touch. I suppose with the marvels of the internet, I could find out.

I did find Robyn, as we hooked up on email several years ago. She lives in Alberta and has two grown kids. We have reminisced about the old days.

My current Jewish friends are in my writing group at Beth Tikvah Synagogue. I am learning about Jewish culture, history and the Jewish sensibility in writing. I look forward to learning more. I have been welcomed with open arms from the start, and I am so blessed.

My friend, Raizie brought me to the group. I hope I am a lifer.

In my writing, I take inspiration from my life and those of my fellow writers. In the sacred walls of the synagogue each week, a transformation takes place. I am an honorary Jew.

My husband has suggested I do a parody of Dylan Thomas' famous poem, A Child's Christmas in Wales. This parody would be based on another parody of Thomas' poem by Howard Engel called "A Child's Christmas in Scarborough." Mine would be called A Goy's Chanukah in Thornhill.

My writing group thinks this is a fun idea. I do too, but find myself pondering, "But who is this Goy?" My self-identification as a Jewish writer is near complete. My childhood wish to be part of a Jewish community has come true.

# Day One

*Sam Hoffer*

The ringing of the telephone startled her. Only Boris knew Sara's number.

"Is everything in order?" asked the familiar voice on the other end.

"Yes."

"I've reserved seats 5 and 6 in Row G at the opera." He hung up. Anything more could betray them. Sara ached to talk to him, but this was not the time.

In her copy of Thomas Hardy's *The Return of the Native* she turned to page 7, corresponding to the place of the letter G in the alphabet and found line 5. She memorized the words. She would look for them and the coded message in today's issue of Le Monde, in the personal section. She closed the website and her laptop, then put on her coat. It had rained in the morning and it was still threatening.

"Come Gigi," she called. She had been assigned the dog by Boris, in charge of their Paris mission. He had told her that the three-year-old Toy Poodle was trained and came from the kennel of a Mossad operative, its clinging nature ideal for Sara's needs. Gigi was a necessary cover he had explained, but under no circumstances was she to endanger herself or the operation to save the dog if things went wrong. Gigi had been dropped off at her apartment by a young man she had never met and who did not introduce himself. Alone with the dog, she had proceeded cautiously, more than a little skeptical of how this would turn out. She was not a dog lover and had never owned a pet.

They walked down the hall toward the elevators, Sara listening for any sounds that might reveal a watchful eye. She stepped onto the cobbled street, continuing in the direction of the intersection where the newspaper stand was always a hub of activity. As she rounded the corner, she deliberately stopped at the baker's stall and asked for a croissant. She continued on, bought a newspaper and casually flipped through the sections, pretending to check the headlines.

"Let's go home, Gigi," she said, stuffing the folded newspaper into her bag. She hesitated, noticing the pleading look in Gigi's eyes and broke off a tiny piece of the croissant. Gigi swallowed it whole and looked up at Sara, hoping for more.

Ahmed noticed the woman from his seat at a small table in front of the cafe across the street. He sensed an alertness in the woman's manner. He kept his eyes on her as she bought her pastry and proceeded to pick up a newspaper. Although the presence of the dog made him somewhat uncertain, there was a stiffness about the way she treated it that added to his suspicion. Could she be part of the Mossad team that they expected would retaliate against the recent bombing of the Jewish community center?

His superiors had long believed that the Israelis kept a safe house in the area. He had been posted here to observe, his instructions clear: locate and report, do not engage.

With a nod to Farid at the cash register, he moved cautiously in the direction of the woman before she slipped away.

Sara felt eyes on her. She wasn't sure from where but it was the instinct that had saved her before. She wouldn't look around, forcing herself to stay focussed on behaving normally, though every nerve was on edge. She walked to the corner, retracing her footsteps. When she was out of view of the intersection, she turned again and quickly entered a small laneway. It would have to do, even if it was a dead-end.

She gathered Gigi in her arms, praying that she would not betray them and slid behind the metal dumpster parked along the wall. She reached for her pistol.

She heard footsteps stop in the laneway where she had turned in. Only feet away from the dumpster. Someone was coming for her. She had nowhere to go.

The silence told Ahmed that she was there, behind the dumpster. Probably armed, but likely protecting her dog. It would give him an edge. He recalled his orders, "do not engage" and hesitated. If he walked on and let her go, he could follow her later. But she would lead him in meaningless directions. He might even lose her. She was trapped. If he captured her, she would make a great prize. He drew his automatic. He had to move in, now.

Sara heard the stealthy approaching footsteps. She threw the croissant to her left.

Gigi instantly leapt after the food as Sara dove around the other side of the dumpster, crouching and firing at the target. Ahmed stared at the dog in disbelief as he absorbed each bullet.  He sank to the ground, his pistol dropping from his hand.

She knew that the man might not be alone. There was no time to retrieve documents from his body. She walked quickly to the end of the laneway, checking to see whether anyone was coming. Not yet, she calculated, although the sound of the shots would have alerted any accomplice the man had. In as nonchalant a manner as she could manage, Sara walked on, Gigi keeping pace at her side. She turned at the first corner drawing any followers away from the direction to her apartment. She would have to contact Boris to alert him to what had happened and get further instructions. If her cover was blown, her entire mission might change. Her stomach tightened at the thought that she hadn't even read the coded message in Le Monde.

The dog had been a good cover she thought, but if someone had seen them, they would be more visible now. She picked Gigi up and quickened her pace. The dog's head grazed her cheek. She glanced down and it instinctively looked up at her.

"I owe you one, Gigi," she heard herself say, astonished at her own words.

# Ben's War

*Fiona Gold Kroll*

*There's a valley in Spain called Jarama / It's a place that we all know so well / It was there that we gave of our manhood / And many of our brave comrades fell. / We are proud of the British Battalion / And the stand for Madrid that they made / For they fought like true sons of the people / As part of the Fifteenth Brigade.*
*From "Jarama Valley / Song of the British Battalion"*

Ben lay sprawled on the ground. He raised his hand to the bullet hole in his chest and felt warm blood trickle from his body. He heard Sophie's footsteps on the dirt, running towards him.

"Hang on, hang on!" she called.

Sophie dropped to her knees and took his hand. He knew he was dying. Spending his final moments with the woman he loved made it easier to let go. He felt at peace. His muscles relaxed. He closed his eyes, Sophie's face etched in his memory as he drew his last breath.

An idealist, Ben couldn't tolerate people who complained about the fascists and did nothing. Once he conned his way into one of Oswald Mosley's British Union of Fascist meetings. Ben heckled the speaker until Mosley's goons dragged him outside, punched, kicked and beat him, and left him on the street for dead. For a young man with a weak heart he was lucky to be alive.

But when Mosley announced a protest march through the heart of the Jewish East End of London in October 1936, Ben knew he had to stop them. He and his friends helped set up road blocks and together hundreds of thousands of Jewish and Irish workers marched and chanted, "1,2,3,4,5 we want Mosley dead or alive!"

That day, scores of people were arrested, many others were injured, and hospitalized before 'The Battle of Cable Street' ended in humiliation for Mosley; he and his black-shirts were unable to pass.

But nothing changed. The fascists continued shouting anti-Semitic insults and hurled rocks at Jewish homes and businesses. With more than two hundred thousand Jews living in London, Ben felt they could hold their own against the five thousand members of Mosley's mob. But, that summer Hitler occupied the Rhineland, and the Berlin Olympic games confirmed to the world Germany's racist and anti-Semitic policies. Ben believed that war between Britain and Germany was inevitable. He also knew that if ever conscripted, his weak heart would preclude him from joining the army. As he paced back and forth in his room, he could only focus on what he could do to help stem the rise of fascism in Europe.

He talked with friends and by the end of that year, decided to join the International Brigades and fight against the fascist Franco in the Spanish Civil war. He left a note on the mantle over the fireplace in the parlour.

"I have to do this; I love you all, Ben."

In January 1937 Ben crossed the English Channel and made his way to Paris and then on to Albacete, Spain. There he joined an English-speaking infantry and machine-gun battalion.

He told no one about his weak heart and he looked good; he had enough adrenaline pumping through his veins after each target practice to keep his skin rosy for days.

With troops as ready as they could be, the battle of the Jarama River began on February 6, 1937. The British Battalion took up positions above the valley close to Aganda.

But the Republicans were no match for Franco's army. With heavy losses and the battalion unprotected, the volunteers pulled back to their base.

Disillusioned and on the verge of physical collapse the battalion tried to recapture their position. Ben kept up with the best of them. On one occasion he stormed a trench and came face to face with one of Franco's corporals, whose eyes flashed with the same fear as his own. Ben's heart raced. It was him or the enemy. In the moment that it took the soldier to raise his rifle, Ben lunged forward, his bayonet sinking deep into the soldier's chest. He fell to his knees; Ben rammed his bayonet into the corporal again, and again. The soldier crumpled, blood ran from his mouth and wounds, puddled on the ground and he died. Still holding his gun, Ben's hands shook, his heart pounded; he could barely breathe. Who was this man he had just killed? Tears rolled down his cheeks; he was someone's son.

If there could be another meaning of hell, it was life in the trenches. Rain, mist, damp, cold winds and sludge, day in and day out. Sometimes the water at the bottom took on a life of its own with frogs, and insects looking for lice and fleas that the soldiers picked out of their hair and clothes between gun battles and explosions. Rats ran over the men during the night, as they tried to sleep. The dreaded trench foot was crippling. Their feet swelled so much that the soldiers couldn't feel them, not even a pin prick. And when the swelling did go down, they suffered unbearable pain.

When Ben's feet swelled to the point where he couldn't remove his boots, it took one of his mates and a medic to carry him to an ambulance loaded with casualties. The wounded groaned each time one of the tires dropped into a pothole on the winding dirt road that climbed towards battalion headquarters and the hospital tent overlooking the valley.

They laid Ben on a cot amongst the bleeding and half dead. A nurse came over to him, her white apron smeared in blood. She smiled; her dark eyes penetrated Ben's and he smiled back at her. She looked at his unshaven face, chiseled features, deep set eyes and thick black hair and wrapped her warm fingers around his wrist. "Have you always had a slow pulse?" she said.

"I don't know, he lied. "But my doctor said something about a valve not working properly."

"What's your name soldier?"

"Ben, and yours?"

"Sophie. Close your eyes and rest until the doctor comes. We have to get those boots off your feet and it's going to hurt."

"Will you be here?"

Sophie slipped her hand around Ben's, squeezed it and walked away.

Ben fell asleep in a horizontal position for the first time in weeks. When he stirred, Sophie stood over him and wiped his face with a damp cloth. His head groggy, he felt like he had been asleep for days.

"You've got a nasty case of trench foot," the doctor said.

"It's going to hurt like hell when we cut those boots off, and I don't have anything to give you except a few swigs of Port. First, let's have a listen to your ticker."

The doctor bent down and moved the cold stethoscope around Ben's chest, first the front and then the back.

"How did you manage to volunteer? You know, you have a weak heart," said the doctor.

Ben shrugged his shoulders. "Let's get those boots off."

Ben drank as much Port as he could handle and lay down. Sophie held his hand.

The pain wasn't too bad while the doctor cut the leather away from his ankle. Then he began to pull— slowly. His torn socks exposed raw, red blisters and black dying skin. He yelled out when the pain became too bad. Sophie stroked his head and wiped beads of perspiration from his forehead. By the time the doctor removed the last boot, Ben's face was white, translucent like porcelain.

"I don't know if we'll be able to save your feet or if you will ever walk again. We'll know in the next day or two," said the doctor.

The doctor picked up Bens chart, scribbled a few words and handed it to Sophie before he hurried away.

Sophie let go of Ben's hand. "Don't leave me."

"I won't. I have to dress your wounds."

Though it took several days, Ben's feet began to heal, the swelling subsided and his numb toes came back to life. With Sophie on one side and a cane in his other hand, Ben walked again. They talked and laughed together and whenever they could Ben and Sophie found a private moment to hold one another and kiss. They were in love.

The war continued on with disastrous numbers of casualties. In February, the Americans arrived and formed the Lincoln Battalion, and by the end of the month, battle plans were drawn to recapture lost positions. Ben wanted to return to his post. He could walk, he felt strong, but he needed clearance from the doctor.

"I can't let you go back to the front Ben."

"Why not?"

"You may feel well, but your heart is weaker than ever. I've sent a message to your commanding officer. You can head back to your battalion and receive your discharge papers tonight."

"But"—

The doctor stood up and put his hand on Ben's shoulder.

"It's time to go home, soldier."

Ben picked up his belongings and walked outside holding Sophie's hand.

"For selfish reason's I'm pleased you're going home," she said.

Ben kissed her neck and eyelids.

"I wish you were coming with me," he said.

"I'll be back in London soon. I want to meet your brothers, all your family. And my mother, my mother will love you!"

Ben removed the Chai and chain from his neck. "Sophie, wear this for me."

"Why?" she asked.

"So I know you'll be safe."

"Nothing is going to happen to me."

"I know, but I'll feel better if you wear it until you get home."

Sophie slipped the chain around her neck and kissed Ben one more time. "I'll walk with you a bit further," she said.

"No, there are snipers up here at dusk. Write to me Sophie and don't you dare kiss another man!"

Ben waved before he disappeared down the dirt path through the grass covered knoll and headed towards the sentry at his battalion headquarters. He stopped and showed his papers; the guard let him pass, though not before they shared a few puffs of a cigarette and a joke. Then he walked towards his commanding officer's tent.

Sophie turned and began walking back to the triage unit. Suddenly, she heard a loud crack. She turned and ran down the path. In the distance, Ben lay on the ground.

"No, no!" she screamed.

In March, Sophie returned to London and visited Ben's brother in the East End. She hammered twice on the tarnished brass knocker.

Jacob opened the door. He looked remarkably like Ben. And then the words tumbled out of Sophie's mouth, almost in one sentence.

"Hello, I'm Sophie. I nursed Ben in Spain. I wanted to return his Chai. You know I loved him."

She burst into tears.

Jacob put his arm around Sophie's shoulders and walked her inside the house towards a chair in the parlour.

Ben, he thought. You and your damned ideals.

# Too Close for Comfort

*Raizie Jacobson*

On Monday, August 24, 2009, Joe Corbett was found dead by his own hand in apartment 307 in a 32-unit building in Denver, Colorado.

He was 80 years old and a loner, who woke up early every morning, opened the door a crack and took in his newspaper. At 8 a.m. that morning, the apartment house manager noticed the paper lying on the ground, picked it up and rapped on the door.

Receiving no response, the manager ran back to his office and grabbed a key.

When he opened the door, he found Joe Corbett lying on the floor with a single gunshot wound to the head.

Why is this of interest to me?

In 1960 my husband, my 2-year-old daughter and I lived in our new home in a suburban housing development in Winnipeg, surrounded by good friends and neighbours with their young children and infants.

It was summer and I was in the early stages of my second pregnancy. I was having some complications and my doctor advised me to rest as much as I could, especially while caring for an active toddler.

I rested and read magazines and books, while my child napped.

Meanwhile, my parents decided to rent out the upstairs apartment of their home.

They placed an advertisement in the Winnipeg Free Press and a young man, well-groomed and equally well-dressed arrived at their home in a taxicab with his belongings. My mother, who considered herself a good judge of people, liked what she saw and rented the accommodations to him on sight. She did have some reservations however, because she found it strange that he arrived in a taxi with only a duffel bag and moved in immediately.

They were always telling me what a nice, neat, quiet young man he was and how pleased they were with him as a tenant. He kept to himself and went to the library every day for hours.

One afternoon while my toddler slept, I was reading a Reader's Digest magazine and noticed an article along with a picture of a man who was Number One on the FBI's 10 Most-Wanted list. I recognized his picture immediately. He was my parents' model tenant.

I rushed to their home, magazine in hand and we called the police at once. A detective was assigned to the case and came to interview my parents and to verify that he was the fugitive. By this time, the tenant had also seen the article and slipped away unannounced, leaving behind his meager belongings.

The detective checked out the apartment, including the garbage, and found scraps of paper where Corbett had practiced my father's signature, along with personal information about what my father did and where he banked.

That was the last we heard of Corbett. We never learned of his arrest or anything else about him, and I don't even remember the alias this convict used in Winnipeg. In November, I gave birth to a healthy baby boy, our lives went on and I never consciously thought of Corbett again until recently.

And so you are wondering how I know all this, fifty-five years later?

I could have let the event drift into the past, but I could not help but wonder what happened to Corbett. I took all the information that I had and searched the internet for the FBI's most wanted for 1960.  Corbett's name popped up immediately. Bingo!

That was him. Reading his history after all these years created a fear and a chill in me when I realized what could have happened, and grateful that no harm came to my family. It is hard to believe the nightmares this story produced in me.

I recalled the first time I saw Corbett. He was a young, tall, thin man who wore jeans and a plaid shirt. He was in his early thirties and if you saw him on the street you wouldn't have noticed him at all. He just blended in.

The police always warn people that the most dangerous criminals are, not who you would think they are. It is not the scariest or sinister looking people that we should fear the most. Criminals usually look very ordinary and do not stand out.

I could not believe what I read as Corbett's story unfolded before my eyes.

Corbett had been previously jailed for second degree murder in 1950 where he was sentenced to five years behind bars. He escaped and continued to elude police while carrying out robberies and moving from place to place. He headed north from California.

On Tuesday, February 9th, 1960 in Denver, Colorado, a milk delivery man on his morning rounds discovered his path blocked by a station wagon. It belonged to Adolph Coors III, the 44-year-old chairman of Golden Brewery and grandson of its founder.

Blood spattered on a bridge railing and the discovery of a hat and a pair of glasses belonging to Coors sparked a massive manhunt. The kidnapper mailed a ransom note to Coors' wife with instructions to get five hundred thousand dollars, and then take out a classified ad for a tractor in The Denver Post.

She followed the instructions, but never heard from the kidnapper.

Within days the investigation focused on a man who drove a canary yellow 1951 Mercury seen in the area. He went by the name of Walter Osborne, though he was really Joseph Corbett Jr.

Just over four years earlier, Corbett had walked away from a minimum security prison in California, the same man who vanished the morning after Coors disappeared.

The Mercury turned up in New Jersey, abandoned and set ablaze. Detectives discovered that Corbett had ordered handcuffs, shackles and guns by mail order and bought a typewriter like the one used to write the ransom note.

Seven weeks after the murder, Corbett was added to the FBI's 10 Most Wanted list, and a transcontinental international pursuit unfolded.

While target shooting at a Douglas County dump, a man discovered clothing and an engraved penknife belonging to Coors, and investigators would find his bones scattered in the forest.

The FBI and Canadian detectives picked up his trail in Toronto, where he had left behind chains and padlocks and a copy of "Anatomy of a Murder." How ironic that he chose the book that was turned into a successful 1959 movie about a man accused of murder and found not guilty on the grounds of "irresistible impulse" a version of a temporary insanity defense.

In the book, the lawyer tried to collect his fee, and when he arrived at the trailer park the trailer was missing. The man left a note for the lawyer that he was "seized by an irresistible impulse." Maybe Joe Corbett was hoping Jimmy Stewart would successfully defend him in court and he too would get away with murder.

Corbett was an intelligent young man and realized he had to move along. So he disappeared as quietly as he arrived and eluded police under other assumed names until he was discovered in Vancouver on October 29, 1960, about three months after he disappeared from Winnipeg, and was arrested by two detectives and an FBI agent at the Maxine Hotel. After Corbett was arrested in Vancouver, he was returned to the U.S., tried and convicted of the first degree murder of Adolf Coors III.

In 1980, he was released from prison after serving 19 years. After his release, Corbett spent the rest of his years in Denver, keeping to himself and living as a hermit, unwilling to discuss the murder of Coors of which he maintained his innocence. Was it unspoken remorse for his crimes that made him take his own life at age eighty? We will never know.

I shudder to think of what could have happened to my parents, and I am relieved to know that Corbett is dead and cannot harm anyone ever again.

# The Ancient Synagogue of Barcelona

*Jenny Roger*

I stoop under the low doorway, then take six steps down to reach the level of archaic Roman times. There are only two small connecting rooms, built of stone with vaulted ceilings, but what history lies within them.

I touch the ancient wall, my hand caressing the rough stones. I press harder hoping to feel the spirit of the people who prayed here, their laughter and their tears.

I feel nothing.

I am in the Ancient Synagogue or Sinagoga Major de Barcelona in Catalan which lies in the Gothic Quarter of Barcelona in the area known as the Call. This was the old Jewish Ghetto in Barcelona.

The synagogue ceased to function in 1391 and the building had many uses afterwards. How do we know that it was a synagogue six hundred years later?

Researchers had to rely on clues.

There are special Jewish rules for synagogue construction. Cornerstones must be marked, the building must be oriented facing east towards Jerusalem and there must be two windows also facing Jerusalem that the light passes through after it has travelled from the city of the Holy Temple.

Archaeological excavations date the building back to Roman times. A corner stone had the markings of the number

18 on it, the Hebrew symbol for life, and the position of the walls excavated showed that they faced south west towards Jerusalem. The more modern Gothic portion sitting on top of the Roman walls has two windows facing Jerusalem, fulfilling the requirements of Jewish ritual construction.

Records from a medieval tax collector show that his route ended at that address in front of the synagogue. Put these clues together and you have a synagogue.

At the time of its destruction in 1391 the Jewish community of Barcelona comprised twenty-five to thirty percent of the total population of the city, a substantial number.

I turned and listened to the guide explain that life in the Jewish ghetto in Barcelona, wasn't as difficult as living in the ghetto in Venice, where residents were locked in at night. But they also had severe building restrictions and could only build up, not out, creating the very narrow streets of the Call. All synagogues could be no larger than the smallest church, regardless of the size of the population or need. The meaning of the word Call isn't exactly known, but it is believed to come from the Hebrew for Congregation. I know that the guide tried to make me feel better by stating that the residents of the Call weren't locked in at night. But I felt worse.

I touched the stones again – talk to me – tell me something – I implored them. More silence.

I take a few steps. The guide continues her lecture on Medieval Jewish life in the Call. Although rarely discussed, the Jews enjoyed a vibrant life and played an important role, when travelling through Medieval cities in Europe.

Forbidden to join Guilds, and restricted from owning property, the Jewish people were tradesmen, bankers, and physicians. The Church forbade usury, which allowed Jews to lend money and fill that role. Many Jews became wealthy from banking and trade.

In Spain, the Jews paid their taxes directly to the King not to the Church. When the King wanted to start a war or build a new castle, he would request the money from the Jews. As long as they could provide the funds the King gave the Jews some level of protection.

In 1391 the Black Plague ravaged Barcelona. Yet, fewer Jews died than their Christian neighbours. Rituals require Jews to wash their hands before every meal and bathe once a week in the Mikveh. But, Christians didn't have such rigorous bathing and hand washing rules. The combination of healthy personal hygiene and burying their dead quickly helped protect the Jews from the ravages of the plague.

Not understanding this and with superstition and anti-Semitism running rampant, attacks against Jews occurred across Spain. Four hundred Jews were murdered in Barcelona, the rest of the community fled or were forced to convert to Christianity.

That was known as the early start of the Inquisition.

The Sinagoga Major lost its congregation almost overnight. The building was no longer a synagogue, and reverted to other uses.

I thought about the absolute cruelty of the Inquisition. It became clear why the Middle Ages were also known as the Dark Ages. The Church held onto its power partly through keeping its followers in the dark. The knowledge of reading and writing was confined to clergy members.

In contrast, Jewish men were encouraged to learn to read Hebrew, to follow the Bible and Holy texts. Jewish men were scholars; they also continued to study science and mathematics, and were famous for their knowledge of medicine. Yet somehow all this knowledge was ignored.

My mood darkened while I listened to the guide tell the next story.

Almost one hundred years later a family moved in who were believed to be Conversos, converts who secretly practiced Judaism. With the Inquisition starting up in full force the family decided to flee, all except for the mother-in-law who chose to remain. In the mid fourteen seventies the mother-in-law, the last Jewish resident on the site of the synagogue became the first Jew to be killed by the Inquisition.

My face showed the dismay I felt.

Close to one hundred years after the massacre in Barcelona this poor woman was hunted down.

"Was she burned at the stake?" I asked the guide. "Probably," was the answer.

"Was it in the large courtyard beside the Cathedral?" "Probably," she wasn't sure.

The guide changed the subject and brought us back to the present day. "There are about four thousand Jews currently living in Barcelona," she said.

I exited the synagogue into the narrow street, and joined the throngs of tourists crowding the Gothic Quarter. A few blocks away stands the Cathedral. The Sun shone down on the courtyard and the children played as groups of tourists waited to enter the Church.

In 1492 King Ferdinand and Queen Isabella ordered the expulsion of all Spanish Jews who refused to convert to Christianity. Many fled, many converted, and many were tortured and burned at the stake and their wealth confiscated. Jewish life in Spain came to an abrupt end.

I stood transfixed, thinking of that poor woman burning at the stake, and how cruel people can be, how easily those bad times were forgotten.

Perhaps the stones did talk to me after all.

# Mother knows best: Enlisting her as a waiting room spy

*David Rapoport*

When my late mother Rose appeared in our waiting room, everything got lively, heralded by the buzz of conversation I soon heard from my consulting room. This was a major factor in my office, as she often arrived an hour early, and had to stay long after she was seen by Dr Susan, my associate, a situation dictated by Wheel-Trans transportation logistics. Instead of accepting our invitation into the inner office, she preferred to stay where the action was. While waiting to be seen, she had the ability to charm her ever-changing audience, as patients came and went. She got female patients to chat by her friendly smile and by compliments about their hair styles or clothing.

With older men, she simply asked which doctor they were seeing, and then she asked probing questions if they were seeing me.

Despite my pleas, mom insisted on telling the other patients who she was, after her interview. Predictably, she became an instant celebrity after introductions were made. Then my patients inevitably told mother how wonderful I am. None would dare say anything negative about me, because although mom was short, she was feisty-and on home territory so to speak. In turn, later on, many patients had nice things to tell me about my mother. Really, though, what fool of a patient could criticize his or her doctor's mother? Only those with a death-wish need apply.

As a bonus, mother discussed their various health problems if time permitted, and had an opinion about any ailment yet discovered. She gained the confidence of others by revealing her own ailments, and fairly often there was an exchange of information on treatments. One man even said he could leave without seeing me, as mother seemed to set his complaint in order. She very speedily convinced him to linger, as his departure would be bad for business, saying, "Oh no, please don't leave, my son will get annoyed with me." As it turned out, the man in question may have done better listening to mother, but he survived anyway.

Mom's detective work was simplicity itself. It went this way:

"Whose patient are you?" (She did not carry on this way with my associate's patients).

"For how many years?"

"Does he ever talk about his mother?" "Do you like his care?"

"Do you think that the office runs well?" "How about the secretarial staff?"

(Again) "Does he ever talk about his mother?"

Thus, when we said hello, mother told me the results of her investigation, and revealed which patients were dissatisfied or crabby about a long wait, or who made disparaging grumbles as they left, oblivious to the little secret agent in the corner. Mom was smart enough to steer clear of those more taciturn patients and those who appeared disturbed or peculiar. Every physician has some of these. Later, when she was de- briefed, I got the benefit of her motherly advice about which patient I should be careful with, or even "fire" as soon as possible from my practice. "Lose that guy, he is a real psycho," she'll say, or,

"That sneezing woman is full of germs, put on a mask when you see her."

One day she spotted a young female patient of the sort that can be hazardous to a male physician. She was dressed and made-up seductively, and in short order mom learned that she worked in a massage parlour, and that she had found me cute on an earlier visit. As a preventive measure, mom interrupted me with this news before I even saw the woman, so I kept a staff person in the room during my examinations.

To my surprise and embarrassment, mom carried on her celebrity routine, even while admitted to my hospital. Thus, the entire nursing staff and many of my colleagues were informed of my brilliance and superb clinical skills. By coincidence, she once had a hospital roommate who was my patient, so a lot was said in the few days they were together. This led later on to a great compliment for mother, who was indeed quite youthful looking. My elderly and somewhat near-sighted patient thought that she was my wife.

I did not tell mom about this flattering statement for a while, saving it for the right occasion, to be used as ammunition in the ongoing political strife common to any extended family. Of course, this became a story mom constantly related to her friends.

Besides raising four children and working alongside dad in their grocery store, often with babe in arms, she found time to care for her own parents and in-laws. This gave me my earliest medical knowledge, as they went from stroke to diabetes to coronary heart disease to brain tumour to colon cancer; and from hospital to nursing home to the death of the previous generation. I was lucky enough to have grandparents until my teens and mom was there for them all.

Lest the reader think that my story is unique, I have recently discovered mom did a similar routine when visiting the offices of other doctors and dentists in our family. Mother could not keep her pride a secret, so she expressed it in public relations. This could not hurt, it kept her busy, and she loved it!

Mom died suddenly in 2008 at age 85, suffering an internal haemorrhage. She had lived long enough to be a major influence on her grandchildren, and all but two were present that day. My Israeli brother was phoned and he spoke to her briefly. We like to think that she heard him, but this was doubtful. Her demise took 6 hours, divided by heroic efforts in my hospital's Emergency Department and Intensive Care Unit. Before moving her to the ICU we all had a 5-minute chance to see her still conscious. As we three children and 9 grandchildren quickly paraded in and out, she said, "You all came to say goodbye?"

It was all over 3 hours later, after we spoke to my esteemed surgical colleague in charge of the unit. She told us there was no hope. The elder of my 2 sisters objected to our "letting her go," suspecting that she herself would die of ovary cancer later that horrible year. She cried, "I can't let her go, David, I need her." I am sure that if my sister had died first, mom would have been a tower of strength in my sister's last 4 months. At least mom was spared the ordeal of burying a child.

I have one regret: in that 5-minute window, she asked me for some water, but I told her that the nurse would have to give me permission. Then they took her away, leaving me to feel that I had failed her at the end. I was age 66 and had been a dutiful son to a loving mother. Still--.

Mom had been a widow for 19 years by that time. Dad had always accompanied her to my office, but his presence probably delayed her spying career. Dad's last words to me had been, "Look after your mother, she's a good woman."

When it was all over, we kids were surprised that mom and dad had saved enough over the years to allow my mother to live well and independently. It should not have been a surprise, for it was the product of saving his meagre earnings and their self- denial over many years. It was the immigrant experience, so common to the brave souls who came to Canada from all over the world.

Whenever I visit my parents' graves, I picture them side by side on their front porch, smiling hello and waving goodbye. At graveside, as is customary, I place a stone on their monuments to show someone had visited. If I can manage, I crouch down and whisper to them about all the wonderful things their grandchildren have done. If I can't manage this emotionally, I share a quivering and tearful hug with my brother and surviving sister. The loss of a parent, especially a mother, is devastating after we have taken them for granted for so many years. My advice to readers: Jump in your car, visit your parents if you still have them, and give them a big hug.

# First Flower

*Sam Hoffer*

I saw it then –
Not at a fleeting glance
But truly saw it, in all its splendor
And filled my lungs 'til I could breathe no more.

# Blue Plaid

*Ruth Frankel-Graner*

That summer and fall there were men roaming the north whose children's bellies bulged from hunger, men turned away by the army which would have meant a steady paycheck. They hung around post-offices and general stores hoping to hear about work, willing to do anything for a dime. He's not like them.

No, sir! He has prospects. Scuppered from the job he hated, too restless for school, unlucky with women – though not bad looking, or so he's heard— he has friends, decent ones, artists like himself, and four months of unbroken work have netted him thirty, small oil on wood sketches. With luck, he'll have even more when he transfers them to large canvases.

Too broke for the train, he thumbs a ride south, pays for the journey by letting the driver of the truck chew his ears off, looks impressed when he's shown the jagged scars from the bayonet wounds because he is. They are deep, red, terrible. Fellow was slashed to the bone. "Yep, the Boer War," says his driver, "now that was something!" He looks at his passenger. "When you planning to enlist in this one son? Canada's in all right." "Soon," the younger man croaks. Truth is, he's been turned away by both wars. After that, he pretends to be sleeping the rest of the way to the city.

Home in Toronto, he coaxes a flame in the woodstove, leaves unpacking for the next day, falls asleep exhausted, too tired to cook. He dreams of twisted trees tormented by the wind, galloping waters, mountains pummelled into existence by glaciers, boulders flung aside.  Clouds shift, threaten, darken.  He pounds the pillow, grinds his teeth, moans. So confident only a day ago, now he is certain the critics will scoff. The nightmare worsens. A dark, round shape with eyes and a mouth bobs from tree to tree, like the bouncing ball in a sing-along moving-picture show. But there is no music in the dream, and the face is not smiling. The artist sleeps fitfully, fully clothed, his muddy boots staining the sheets with the dark brown earth of Algonquin Park.

With sunlight the dream slips away. He leaps out of bed, picks up a small oil sketch finished just days ago, stares. Pleased, he looks at another, and another. Turns up the lamp. "What the blazes!" Smack dab in the middle of one small painting, a black smudge, about the size of his thumbprint is ruining a section of the lake and part of the tree trunk. He pushes his hair out of his eyes. How could this have happened?  He'll wear the same collar weeks on end, leave the dinner dishes to rot, but he keeps his carrying cases clean as a whistle. He holds his breath, scrapes the mess down to the wood, prepares his palette, re-paints part of the lake and tree, examines the wooden case which held it all the way back from the Park. It's spotless, empty as a hole in a sock.

Only then does he boil his coffee and oatmeal.

He's pared his landscapes down to essentials. Trees, sky, clouds, water, hills, rocks. But there is much more to them. He begins with "the sorrowful woman," a tree that reminds him of his mother, dishevelled, driven to the edge, but still resolute, compassionate, loving; the landscape behind her is detached, remote, so like his father.

By nightfall the background of the first large painting is almost complete. In bed, he worries that he used the wrong cadmium on the sky, too much ultramarine on the background hills. Is it as good as a Gauguin? Would he like it? He might. What would Picasso say, Van Gogh? Would they sneer, call it too close to decoration? He doesn't sleep well again. He's only as good as the painting he's working on. And that dark, unsmiling ball-face returns to his dreams, lurking from tree to tree.

In the morning he stokes the fire, doesn't bother dressing, turns to the 'mother' painting. What? That black thumbprint has moved there— only larger. It almost looks like a face. The face of a man. He's no bible- thumper like his friend Lawren Harris, or airy-fairy like that other painter, the Frenchie, Odilon Redon. He's heard of the shroud of Turin. What nonsense! There must be a knot or flaw in this section of his canvas.

Again he removes the intruding shape, adds fresh oils, works on the hills and boulders, applies careful strokes of alizarin for what he thinks of as his mother's hair. The pine needles will be filled in after everything else. That face on the ball! Did he recognize it?

He forgets to eat, concentrating again on the branches which twine like the locks of a beleaguered woman. He begins to add a deeper vermilion. Astonished, he sees the dark presence is there again, behind the tree, larger, definitely the face of a man. It can't be a "ghosting," the nuisance that happens when the groundwork for a painting reappears, unwanted. He's painted a lot of faces, pretty ones too, but never on this canvas. He scours away the unwanted face, seals the area with shellac. That should do it! He'll let the company know that they have sold him inferior canvas, but first he has promised that several large paintings will be ready by spring.

He turns the completed painting to the wall. He thinks of it as a portrait reflecting his mother's struggle, the universal battle for survival epitomized in a tree hammered by hostile forces. Hadn't Van Gogh striven for that? He tries not to think of the intruding man's face, to wonder if he's watching again from behind the tree. Not until the end of several months does he turn the painting around. Relief! There is nothing to change. Nothing! On the back of the painting he writes, THE JACK PINE 1917. On the front, he signs his name, TOM THOMSON. He steps back, looks around at its companion painting, his father, bowed by the west wind but not beaten, and all his other paintings. Success!

He awakens trembling the day that his patron's truck will arrive, then freezes. That face has reappeared on The Jack Pine. It is detailed enough that he can see the man's collar, a distinctive blue plaid. In a frenzy, Tom wonders, "What would Monet do?" Only a skilled eye notices Claude's last minute alterations. Scarcely breathing, Tom squeezes a dollop of Viridian onto his palette, adds enough turpentine to render the oil thin enough to dry rapidly, a hint of varnish. The face of the man in the blue plaid shirt disappears. The canvases crowd the truck.

A few weeks later, wonderful news! The critics rave! The Jack Pine sets a new record of appreciation. His other paintings also receive accolades. Tom thinks he knows now what it means to die happy.

In the spring he moves into another cabin in Algonquin Park. This one, on Canoe Lake, belongs to a generous friend who's painting much farther north, asking only one favour in return. "Just canoe to the post-office every so often, and ask for Lawren Harris' mail. That way anyone hanging around there will know somebody lives here, and won't try to settle in."

By early July Tom relaxes a little. He has almost enough sketches to take him through the winter. He is content as never before. Not rich—ninety cents in his pocket, but his bills are mostly paid. He will take a few days off, canoe to the post-office, paddle the lakes, fish, call back to the loons.

He lays the bamboo rod and tin canteen on a boulder at the base of a jack pine on Canoe Lake, leans forward to untie the canoe. He does not see the man waiting behind the pine, a man in a blue plaid shirt, a man crazed with starvation. It had been a cruel and difficult winter, and the drought of spring and summer is no better.  His wife and daughter are near death.  He hangs around the post-office hoping for work, desperate to do anything, learns that a son of the rich-as-Midas Massey-Harris clan, the tractor people, bunks only a few miles away, probably carries a wallet stuffed with greenbacks. Easy pickings! What luck that this chump is right here, in Algonquin Park!

Post Script.

For almost a century the mystery of Tom Thomson's drowning will baffle those who knew of him. He was, after all, a strong swimmer and an expert canoeist.

The answer to their speculation lies in The National Gallery of Canada, in a painting entitled The Jack Pine. Near the base of its trunk, a careful viewer will see that a cluster of pine needles is somewhat too large for the tree. Of course it had to be. Concealed beneath that clump is the face of a man. He is wearing a blue plaid shirt. And he's not smiling.

# Flying Solo

*Gerda Frieberg*

When I was growing up, my aunt who lived in Berlin would occasionally visit my family. My father would pick her up at the airport and I went with him. I was fascinated watching the airplane approach and could not comprehend what kept it in the air. One day, I promised myself, I would learn to fly.

But the dark years of the holocaust cast a shadow of loss and suffering. I spent the postwar years watching over my mother while I established my own life. Several years later, after I immigrated to Canada and when our construction company was well established, I decided that I needed a new challenge. My children, by now teenagers, no longer needed my full attention. What next I thought? And my mind drifted back to flying.

Buttonville airport in Markham was only twenty minutes away from our home. I decided to check it out. I arrived at the airport and immediately signed up for flying lessons. I'd never seen a private plane on the ground. The instructor led me to a Cessna 150.

I looked at this small plane, and thought to myself, "This looks like a mosquito; this will carry two people into the air? Well, it is too late now. Let's go." A childhood dream became reality.

As per Canadian aviation rules, it took twenty flying hours with an instructor before I could fly solo, and after thirty-two hours I passed the private pilot's test. In 1970, as one of sixty-four women pilots from Canada and the US, I took part in an air race from Toronto Island Airport to Nassau in the Bahamas. Arriving in 45th place was not bad for a beginner. But a private pilot's license has some limits. In order to fly in any weather, one must have an instrument rating. I asked my instructor what an instrument rating is and how do you obtain it? "It is the PhD of flying, but I don't know of any woman that is an instrument-rated pilot. I don't think you could make it, he said"

His comment did not surprise me, since I could not even pronounce the word trigonometry. But, I was determined to try.

"Can I book a lesson for tomorrow?" I asked.

A few months later I became the first instrument rated woman pilot in Toronto.

Now the sky was the limit. I flew where eagles didn't dare to fly.

On my next visit to Israel, I rented an airplane at Tel Aviv airport. I flew down to Masada to take some photos. On the way back to Tel Aviv I inadvertently entered Jordanian airspace. Seeing the land of Israel from twelve thousand feet, I realized how small and vulnerable the country was.

I flew my own plane in Canada for several years. I had no fear of flying solo, after all I had been doing that one way or another since I survived the Nazi labour camp of Oberalstadt, so many years before.

# Poppies

*Fiona Gold Kroll*

Albert, who often disappeared to Paris for several days at a time, left the house two days ago. This time, he was tense when I asked where he was going.

"To Paris, on business—"

"Are you having an affair?"

"No, I'm not!"

He grabbed his bag and stormed out. But I knew he had a mistress. I smelled her on his clothes each time he returned home.

For now, I didn't want to think about Albert or that woman in Paris. I glanced at my son, the only real joy in my life.

"Maman, can we go for a walk?"

"I'll race you to the meadow," I said.

Together we ran from the house and through the garden until we reached the field and collapsed on the ground in laughter. Émile waved his head from side to side, imitating the vivid red poppies that danced around us in the wind. Breathless, hot, I unclipped my hat, placed it on the ground and shook free my curls.

"We had better walk back, Émile, Anna will have lunch ready."

My son pouted but then looked at me with a mischievous grin. He pulled on my hands until I stood up, and together we walked up the hill. In the distance I glimpsed a heavyset, bearded man with paint brushes in one hand, a palette in the other. He stepped back and with narrowed eyes studied the canvas resting on an easel. For a brief moment our eyes met.

"Who is that?" asked Émile.

"I don't know."

Tired when we reached the house, I asked Anna to take Emile and wash his hands. I sat down at the kitchen table, which was draped in white linen. Thick slices of bread covered the oval bread board, alongside platters of cheese, sliced meats, pâté and green and black olives floating in olive oil. A large blue and white bowl brimmed with luscious red plums, grapes and watermelon slices. Anna prepared a plate for Émile and poured me a glass of wine.

Inside the house, the air was warm and heavy. The wind had dropped and the sky had turned grey. The back of my neck was moist so I pinned my hair back up and unbuttoned my blouse at the neck. I carried my wine and a plate of food outside and sat in one of the wicker chairs on the covered porch. I watched as rain pounded the gravel path. Suddenly a cool wind came up and blew the rain into my face. I shivered, dabbed myself dry with a napkin and pulled the lace shawl lying on the back of the chair around me.

I broke off a piece of cheese and put it to my lips, but placed it back on the plate; I had no appetite. We were deeply in debt. Ostensibly, Albert had gone to Paris to borrow money from his father, but I also knew he would use the trip to spend time with his lover. These days financial worries consumed me, yet Albert seemed indifferent to our predicament and my emotions.

The night before he'd left for Paris, Albert drew me to him, ran his fingers through my hair and tried to kiss me, but I pulled away when he told me he loved me. I had heard those words before, except now they had little meaning. I didn't trust him. I felt betrayed and empty.

Émile came running onto the porch. "Maman, where are you?"

"I'm here, darling." I scooped him up and twirled him around above my head while he squealed with delight. "The rain has stopped. Let's go down to the river. We can pick some flowers and play with your boat."

Émile jumped up and down. "Yes, yes, I'll get my boat," he yelled.

"Anna, we're going to the river, we'll be back soon."

I plopped a hat on Émile's head before he ran across the lawn with his yellow sailboat tucked under one arm. Steam rose from the path where large pots of irises bordered flowerbeds crammed with lilies and sunflowers. Moisture dripped from leaves and petals while the sun fought its way from behind the clouds. As I began my descent down the path, I opened my parasol and called out, "Wait Émile…wait for me."

Albert met his father in Paris at a café on St. Germain. But the meeting did not go well; his father was furious.

"You think you will become a famous writer, but I've yet to see anything of yours in print. For god's sake, man, you have a wife and child. Get a job and support your family!"

"But my manuscript is almost finished and—"

"You've been saying that for the past five years. This is the last time I'm helping you!"

His father stood up, slapped a cheque on the table, set his straw hat on his head and trudged off.

Albert was shocked, unable to move. His first instinct was to tear up the cheque. How could Father speak to me like that, he thought. But he had never seen his father so angry. He realized that if he didn't pull his life together, he and his family could lose their home; he might even lose his wife and son. He looked at his watch. There was just enough time to collect his things from Simone's apartment before catching the train home.

Albert opened the door to the apartment, gathered all his clothes together and packed his bag. He was anxious to leave before Simone returned. He looked at her bed, the place where they had made love the previous night. He remembered the light touch of her fingers when she ran her hand across his chest, her lips that searched the hollows of his body, and her luminous blue eyes that drew him to her. But he knew it had to end. He left her a note propped up beside the pendulum clock on the mantel, locked the door and slid the key underneath.

Albert walked to the station. He needed to clear his head. Paris in August seemed empty. Wives and children had left for the country to escape the oppressive heat in the city. He felt relieved that he had ended his liaison with Simone, and now he looked forward to returning home to Suzanne and Émile and the wildflowers beside the Seine in Argenteuil.

Émile and I wandered down the path through the cornfields until we reached the riverbank. The last of the clouds had dispersed over the horizon; the sky was blue and the sun hot. I wanted to lie beneath the shade of a tree, but the ground was still damp from the rain. Wooden benches lined the riverbank and I sat down, closed my eyes and inhaled the scent of moist grass, blue cornflowers and red poppies.

Émile busied himself tying the sails on his boat and then leaned over to place it in the water.

"Émile, I'm going to pick some flowers. Would you like to help me?"

"No, I want to play with my boat."

"All right, but be careful on the edge of the river. It's slippery."

"I will, Maman."

I carried my basket and scissors a short distance up the hill into the field. A light breeze came up and the poppies turned and nodded to one another as though in lively conversation. Flowers are resilient, I thought. They endure torrential rains, the blazing sun, powerful winds and freezing temperatures—all elements that make them strong and, sometimes, kill them. Perhaps I, like most humans, was no more than a flower struggling to survive.

But merely surviving wasn't enough for me. It was then I decided to try to resolve my problems with Albert. A vase of poppies to welcome him home would be a good beginning. Albert loved them; they'd inspired him to write his book.

I looked over towards the artist I'd seen earlier and caught a glimpse of his canvas. I could just make out blue sky, puffs of white clouds, a blur of red, and in the foreground what might have been a figure. I bent down to pick another poppy.

With my mind on Albert and our difficulties, I had lost track of time, and when I lifted my head I saw that the painter was gone. I realized I couldn't see my son.

"Émile?" I called out. "Émile!"

I ran down to the river. There was no sign of him or his little yellow sailboat. I saw only his brown sandals lying in the grass. Panic took over my mind and body. For a moment I thought I heard Émile calling me. His voice was weak and muffled. I ran up and down the bank of the river, screaming his name. Then I saw him in the water, hanging on to a large rock beside the bridge.

"Don't move, Émile, I'm coming!"

Although I could not swim, I threw my shoes on the grass and leaped into the river. A small knot of people had gathered on the bridge. Two men shouted to me, ran down the grassy bank and plunged into the water, but all I could think of was saving my son. I grabbed onto an overhanging branch, grazing my hands as I struggled to pull myself towards him. But the water came up to my chin and the current fought my every step. No matter how hard I tried, I could not reach Émile. I grew tired, unable to keep my head above the water. As I began to choke, I felt someone grab the back of my collar. It was Albert.

"Émile," I whispered. I felt light-headed, and everything turned black. When I opened my eyes, I was in bed. Albert sat in a chair beside me, unshaven, his face ashen. I tried to sit up, but I was too weak. "Émile?"

Tears filled his eyes.

"He's dead, Suzanne, we couldn't save him."

I felt my heart pound. Blood surged through every vein in my body. I sat up and threw myself at Albert. I slapped his face hard, pummeled his arms with both fists and screamed "No!" Albert grabbed my wrists and I crumpled to the floor on my knees, buried my face in his lap and sobbed.

After Émile's funeral we moved to Haute-Îsle, about seventy kilometers away. Albert never visited Paris again, except for meetings with his agent. His first book, Poppies, was published to critical acclaim.

And me? Sometimes I think I hear Émile call my name. I used to worry that I would forget what he looked like, but his beautiful face is forever etched in my memory. Albert wants to have another child; maybe someday. For now, I'll grow flowers in our garden. Irises, peonies, roses, and more. I did not plant poppies, but last year two sprang up among the dahlias. Albert believes they are a sign that memories can appear in unexpected places. To me their redness felt like a wound that gnawed at my heart like a knife turning slowly, and in the end I chose to leave the poppies in the ground. Will I ever be able to forgive myself for Émile's death? Not even I can say.

# The World's Oldest Food Blogger

*Jenny Roger*

Betcha think I must be at least 90 years old to be the world's oldest food blogger.

Nope, you're wrong. I'm sixty. That can't be you say? Only 60? The world's oldest? Come on.

My unscientific analysis making me the world's oldest food blogger is based on the food events in Toronto I have attended where I always appear to be the oldest person there.

I am referring to people who are bloggers, not cookbook authors or food writers who also have blogs.

There are some in their early fifties and alright, I admit it, I do know an older one who lives in another country and is closer to 80 than 60, but I'm probably the oldest food blogger in Toronto, most definitely in Thornhill, where I live.

And I caught you with my catchy title, didn't I – that's what we're supposed to do.

Most of the food bloggers are pretty young things in their twenties and thirties.

They are energetic, talented and have boundless amounts of energy. They can stand hours perched on high heels dressed in the latest LBD (little black dress) tweeting, Instagramming and liking at the same time. Their make-up and hair of course is always perfect.

While I (in my sensible orthopedic shoes) am busy pressing send on my iPhone over and over hoping the photo will go to its rightful home on the World Wide Web.

But nothing can happen before I choose between different options I don't understand and getting asked for passwords. Which option do I want? Which flaming password do I use? If the definition of insanity is doing the same thing over and over and expecting a different outcome, then at that moment I am qualified as clinically insane don't you think? If not insane, then at least stupid for not figuring it out.

How can the pretty young things do it?

They can interpret their analytics, increase their views, upload, download, post, host, friend, unfriended, hashtag, pin, link, photobomb, and snapshot without batting an eyelash. As a food blogger, I do not even enter into discussing the technicalities of taking photographs, cooking the food and styling it to its most fashionable permutation for the moment.

And they are the true masters of the selfie. You know what I'm talking about don't you?

BTW, IMO ICYMI IDK if my SEO is Gr8 FWIW, LOL. Okay, I know, you want me to translate this into English. Here it goes: By the way, in my opinion, in case you missed it, I don't know, if my search engine optimization, is great, for what it's worth, laugh out loud.

Sometimes I have problems knowing what to say to the bloggers I meet. I'm old enough to be the mother of most of them. Would you want to hang around with your mother at every cool event? I don't think so.

I'm not sure how I've gotten away with being a Toronto food blogger when I don't even live in Toronto. You know how impressed these Toronto people get when they hear you are from the northern region of 905 don't you? Besides, it's a schlep to drag downtown often at rush hour, carrying heavy camera equipment. But all the main action happens in Toronto so that's where I go.

Recently I've been trying to figure out the way forward. Should I give up blogging completely and leave it to the young ones? Or should I see if I can cut back without losing my marketability completely? Should I stop using all social media? Will I be able to go to a restaurant or cook a meal without Instagramming it? Could my husband eat his meal without asking permission first or will I need to Tweet it? You know what I mean?

These are all serious questions I am contemplating.

But then I go somewhere and the excitement kicks in. I go to a restaurant and its celebrity chef owner is there and I get to take his photo. Or I may discover a new artisanal food being produced locally and, you guessed it – more shots.

Will I end up taking photos that aren't very good, even though I appear to look like I know what I am doing? Sometimes when I pull out my camera, strangers will ask me if I am a professional photographer. LOL (you remember this one – Laugh Out Loud). These digital cameras are very complicated little pieces of equipment, and it takes time to learn all the options they have. Needless to say I'm still learning. I read the instruction manual over and over and not a word of its technical jargon makes any sense to me.

Food looks best when it is photographed under natural lighting, no flash allowed. But it is complicated when there isn't enough light, which usually is the case indoors where most stores and restaurants are!

When taking a photo in low light I have to make sure my aperture is large enough so I can use a quick shutter speed while retaining a good focal point, but if I bump my ISO (don't ask) too high then there will be too much noise (graininess)...

Maybe I'm not crazy or stupid after all, maybe I'm just a food blogging addict.

Anybody know of a food blogging addict self-help group? Just DM (direct message) me if you do.

# The Winner

*Carol Green*

Hatred has no direction
Like a balloon let go
It flies around in
Crazy arcs
Its purpose none

Even when targeted
It makes mistakes
Collateral damage

Hate never wins
Though it hits often
It seems to succeed;
That is the irony

Love – gentle, noble, wise,
Humble even,
Triumphs
Every time

Sure-footed,
Patient,
Knowing its direction
Its places assured.

Love is:
Personal
Continual
Everywhere and
Everlasting.

# Gentle Paces

*Sam Hoffer*

He navigated absentmindedly through the crowd at his customary Starbucks, across from City Hall. Although he recognized many of the faces, he was grateful that no one knew him. It allowed him to prolong his waking slumber for a few minutes more before he had to admit that the day had actually begun. Through his mental haze he noticed the woman at the condiments stand reaching for her cup, momentarily distracted by something she saw outside the window. He watched motionless as the back of her hand struck the side of the cup, knocking it over. He sprang into action trying to save the drink, but failed and apologized. Their eyes met.

"I'll get you another cup," he offered.

"Please no, don't bother. It was my fault. I'm already late for work."

"No," he replied, "please wait here."

He made his way to the counter and ordered two coffees. Moments later, he returned. She was still standing where he'd left her.

"I got myself one too," he said, smiling, "so don't feel bad. Would you like to sit down? I also bought us a couple of chairs."

She laughed, thinking, why not, as they both revisited the condiments stand. He had been kind enough, more in tempering her embarrassment than in getting her coffee, though that too was a generous gesture. He had a reserved casualness that set her at ease, but his appearance left her somewhat uncertain. She noted that he wore a pale green t-shirt with no markings and weathered but clean blue jeans. His shoes, however, told a different story.

Originally white, his runners were thick with the grime of the street.

He saw her glance at his shoes, but said nothing. She was a picture of perfection, her long brown hair falling straight beside her bright, oval face, its tanned complexion made more dramatic still by her sparkling brown eyes. He could see without staring that unlike him, she wore brilliant white tennis shoes and socks that fit perfectly with the rest of her appearance.

"I like this place," he declared as they took their seats, "I've been coming here for years." She didn't reply but he instantly sensed that she must be wondering the obvious. "Oh, it's not a hangout, it's where I come to think about my writing. It's a great place for that."

"Oh, you're a writer," she remarked.

He smiled, affirming what he'd said, enjoying the obvious relief in her voice.

"One of those, yes."

"Sorry, I didn't mean..."

"No, it's OK," he interrupted. "With shoes like these, who knows?"

They both laughed heartily.

Still enjoying the moment he said, "I'm Dennis."

"I'm Jackie," she replied. They held each other's gaze for just a moment, both keenly aware that they were strangers.

"And where do your shoes take you, Jackie?" he asked, exaggerating a raised eyebrow.

"Oh, nothing as interesting as writing, but I do read a bit. Mostly political reviews to keep our clients informed of news that is relevant to their enterprise. It's hard for executives to keep up and get a picture of what's going on these days. We try to do it for them."

"Fascinating. But it sounds like you're not giving yourself enough credit. Your writing must be superb to be able to consolidate the masses of information into a meaningful text."

She smiled at his observation. It was true. Their agency lived and died by the quality of the team's analysis.

He caught her just then, glancing at her watch. "I should get going," he said, pretending he hadn't seen anything.

"Yes, I have to go too," she replied as they both got up to leave.

"My office is just around the corner," she said, as they left the coffee shop.

"I'll walk you to the light," he offered, "and then I'm plunging into the masses down there." He pointed in the direction of the intersection congested with pedestrians.

"I enjoyed the chat," he continued. "I hope we can spill some coffee again some time."

"I don't come here every day," she said. "But," she added, "Friday morning coffees are a must. It helps me get the weekend going early."

"See you then," he smiled and waved as she rounded the corner.

# Two Petals Lost

*Carol Green*

It is late summer, and this morning my street is buzzing with activity. Gardeners are out clipping hedges, cutting grass, and whipper-snipping the edges of lawns. It is perfect weather – sunny and warm, but not too warm, and not a cloud obscuring the sun. Sitting at my laptop on our deck, I gaze up at the sun as I type, despite my Mother's admonition to never stare at it. This energizes me.

My garden is full of flowers, most of them in giant pots spread around our property on a steep ravine lot. I planted a few flowers in the ground, like brilliant red geraniums at the side of the house. There is a sink hole at that spot, and the flowers anchor the earth, while providing a glorious burst of scarlet well into the fall. Lilies-of-the-valley share their bed, and when the flowers bloom in spring, they release my favourite scent. I wear lily-of- the-valley perfume, an old-fashioned choice that is hard to find. I prefer the French name *Muguets des Bois*.

Many colourful flowers are in the giant pots mentioned above; on the high deck off the back of the house where I now sit, under the deck, along walkways and on the front steps.

Later in the day, as I walk on the path toward the house, the bright yellow flowers of a hibiscus greet me. They compete for my attention with the fuchsia-coloured blooms of a diplodenia, a new species that is popular at the moment. Cerise snapdragons hover nearby. They have bloomed all summer. (In case you haven't noticed, I love colour).

Our front steps face south, and it is here that my lemon and lime "trees" spend the temperate months. We have four lemons and five limes growing. My husband pollinated them indoors last winter. I wonder if this might be a first for Ontario, to have fresh citrus fruit in our climate. I should probably take photographs. Dancing around my head are visions of key lime pie (and of course, lemon meringue pie).

Last winter, my husband learned that humans can do the bees' work of pollinating by manually spreading the pollen inside each citrus flower. He did so, without telling my son or me. To our great surprise, the flowers gave way to fruit, and the fruit continued to grow. (The unfertilized fruit normally drops off and dies). When the fruit was well on its way, my husband confessed that he was the "bee".

I used to own two other citrus trees: an orange and a tangerine. Our house is not that big inside and we had four citrus trees indoors in the winter. My husband gave me an ultimatum that some of the citrus trees would have to go or he would. I thought about saying, "Bye, it's been nice," but decided instead to choose among my citrus "children" and find the ones I could part with to a good home with visitation rights. Our next door neighbours love plants. I gifted them with the orange and tangerine trees.

In time, my neighbours faced the same difficulty with space for the trees in their house. They asked if I minded if they gave them to their Temple. I gave my blessing, as it was a lovely environment and many people could enjoy them this way. They might even yield fruit the congregants could eat. The orange trees lived out the rest of their days in the atrium of Sanatan Mandir Cultural Centre.

My outdoor potted collection will soon have to move inside. In fact, I have already brought in a few tender cacti and an aloe vera. My hibiscus continues to thrive, although I noticed an aging bloom with two petals lost as I strolled by today. Nature has its ways of shedding the old and moving on. I guess I do too, as I look forward to planning my next garden season, even I as enjoy the last blooms of summer.

# Vilna Vegetarian

*Jenny Roger*

"Look at that!" I called out realizing I was talking to myself out loud.

I was reading an online review of The Vilna Vegetarian, a Jewish vegetarian cookbook originally published in 1938 before World War II. My great-grandmother came from a small shtetl (Jewish village) near Vilna and I was curious to see if I could find any connection with the cookbook and what little I knew of my great-grandmother's cooking. I was also fascinated to read about Jewish vegetarian life in Eastern Europe before World War II.

Cookbook author Fania Lewando along with her husband Lazar Lewando owned a Kosher vegetarian restaurant in Vilna, Lithuania. Vilna was a famous center of Jewish learning and culture in Eastern Europe before World War II. I think of the narrow streets and alleys in the heart of Vilna. I imagine what the busy restaurant may have looked like. Perhaps with wooden floors, tables and chairs placed beside windows looking out onto the busy street in the Jewish section in the center of the city. I imagine a buzz in the air while patrons eat, laugh, and argue in Yiddish with family and friends. Close by, the large synagogue's clocks on the outside of the building showed prayer times, the beginning and end of the Sabbath along with candle lighting times. The guest book from her restaurant records that artist Marc Chagall and Yiddish poet Itzik Manger ate there.

The story of Fania and Lewando ended like millions of other Jews, in tragedy. After unsuccessful attempts to obtain visas to England or the United States, Fania and her husband were captured by Soviet soldiers in 1941 while they were fleeing the Nazis. All trace of them disappeared after that.

Decades later in the United States Barbara Mazur and Wendy Waxman discovered one of the few remaining copies of this cookbook in the YIVO Yiddish Institute for Jewish Research archives in New York City. They showed it to noted American cookbook author Joan Nathan, who then got Shocken Books on board to publish an English translation of the book.

Why vegetarian cooking? The very complex laws of Kashrut call for the separation of dairy and meat, making vegetarian recipes an important part of the diet. There is also a spiritual element to the vegetarian part of the Kosher diet in refraining from killing animals for food.

Fania felt it was a very healthy way to eat, recognizing the value of the vitamins obtained from eating vegetables. She recommended that the produce "must be of the highest quality" and to use clean utensils. Noting that her recipes be followed exactly because she had tested each one several times, Fania wanted her cookbook to be one that housewives would actually use.

The book was written in the style of older cookbooks of which there are over four hundred recipes and only brief cooking instructions. It was natural to assume that all women knew how to cook in that era. Wood burning stoves were used and it was impossible to give exact directions for cooking because there was no way to tell exactly what the temperature of the stove or stove top was.

I started to recognise a few recipes my great-grandmother would have made.

One was the Cheese Salad which mixed Farmer's (dry cottage) Cheese with sour cream, diced green onion and salt and pepper. It was eaten with black bread. That was one of my grandfather's favourite lunches, only he would enjoy it best if his green onion had a huge strong bulb attached to it, the stronger and more pungent the onion, the better.

Another recipe was one my grandmother's sisters used to make which I had forgotten about, Potato Soup with milk, consisting of blanched potatoes with onions, salt and pepper cooked in milk. It brought back memories of my great-aunts in their tiny kitchen in their apartment on Bathurst Street busily cooking away while talking up a storm, so happy to have company. They always added green peas and carrots to the soup, and served it with the best fresh rye or pumpernickel bread from the nearby Hamishe Bakery.

Vegetarian cooking made sense in pre-war Eastern Europe. Kosher meat became more and more difficult to obtain as anti-Jewish laws took effect coupled with rising poverty making meat unaffordable. But Fania Lewando's book would be perfectly at home in today's modern kitchen as people are gaining interest in vegetables. The health food movement was alive in Eastern Europe long before World War II. It was only in the 1960's that it started its revival again in North America.

Many of the modern day trendy vegetarian recipes have quinoa, ancient grains, lots of spices and exotic ingredients. This is a great book for people who enjoy more traditional Western flavors and produce.

It is also a beautiful snapshot into a lost time, showing how much had been destroyed by the Nazis in World War II.

Fortunately, with the publication of The Vilna Vegetarian we have been able to recover a lost gem.

At least twenty years have passed since I last saw my great aunts make this soup. It is a humble soup, not very expensive to make and containing only a few ingredients. I'm sure in times of poverty this soup eaten with a chunk of bread would have made the entire meal.

My aunts simply called it "Milchig Soup," Milk Soup. I have combined both Fania's and my great aunts' recipes together in the recipe below.

*Milk Soup (Potato Soup with Milk)*
2 lbs. peeled and finely diced potatoes
1 tablespoon butter
1 onion, finely diced
1 or 2 carrots, finely diced
4 cups milk
Salt, pepper
Handful of frozen green peas

Blanch the diced potatoes in a pot of boiling water for three minutes.

Drain, reserve the potatoes. Return the pot to the stove and over medium low heat melt the butter. Add the onions and cook gently, stirring for about three minutes. Add the carrots and cook for one more minute. Return the potatoes to the pot, and add the milk. Bring the milk almost to a boil so that the milk around the edges of the pot shows little bubbles. Add the salt and pepper. Stir the vegetables. Cover and keep it on a very low simmer, not a boil for 30 minutes. The milk could easily burn if you boil it.

After about 20 minutes when the potatoes are tender, add the frozen green peas.

Let them heat up in the soup for a few minutes and the soup is ready to serve.

So try this simple soup, it's vegetarian, it's gluten free and it is comfort food at its best.

# SPINACH WRAP at The True Blue Wooden House Restaurant

*Ruth Frankel-Graner*

Jennifer leans over the counter to get closer to her boss. "I asked her like you said Steph, that lady in the red sweater at table number three. I said, "Did you like your dinner?" She said she didn't like the spinach wrap. She called it spinach crap."

Stephanie at twenty-three, is four years older than her summer helper. She is peeling cello wrap from day old macadamia nut, white chocolate-chip cookies, arranging them on leaves of iceberg lettuce in overlapping circles on a platter painted with strawberries; dots them with rose radishes, places them beside the cash register, stands back to admire the effect. One of the radishes is a little out of line.

"Jen hon, when you've been at this as long as I have, you'll learn that you just can't please everyone. Some days, you can't please anyone."

She looks over at the lady in the red sweater. "That babe's probably a free loader hoping we won't charge her because she complained. Wait a few minutes, and then hand her the bill."

The sole occupant of table three is tonguing tea. This is her first visit to Historic True Blue Wooden House Restaurant. The tea is barely hot enough, and she had requested Roibos.

It came in a little printed paper bag, ruinous to the known delicacy of Roibos. And the pot itself was badly proportioned—spout and handle all akimbo, interior coated with inferior, Jiangzu Province clay, imparting a disconcerting bitterness. Rita Jaquard, Jack the Rita to some, columnist for Gourmand Plaisir Magazine (International) records in her small black binder, "My first meal at The Historic True Blue Wooden House Restaurant. Well, there's a mouthful right there! It's rumoured that Prime Minister Sir John A. tarried here. What on earth for!"

This ensnarement in the northern wilds of Ontario is the coup de main of Rita's insatiable editor. Her true arrondissement is Toronto, Montreal, Vancouver. Big cities, big chefs. But a new generation of foodie kids, petites frites weaned on tomatoes farcies a la Portugaise, who have hobnobbed with Veal Prince Orloff, summer camped in kitchens in Boulogne or Nicoise, have pushed her below the salt.

She continues her note-making. "Here it is, rainiest summer on record, and I am in the piney, slimy (cross that out,) woods of Northern Canada: to wit, the picturesque, one might even say picaresque hamlet of Milton Mills. But if Sir John did lunch here, it was no doubt to his regret. The restaurant is a fake, a fraud, a poseur of the most inedible order. There are five tables in the entire Auberge, petit fours of small overly polished squares of pine, skewered on wrought (as in overwrought) iron pedestals, patterned after frangipani (!!!) leaves. Need I say more? Well, all right. It gets worse. The ancient walls have been skinned to conceal every hint of their past." She hesitates; perhaps scalped reads better—a subtle reference to Canada's past. No too controversial. She gets in enough hot water as it is. "And what can be said about an old building, old at least by Canadian standards, to which a mere pastiche of artifacts— chipped flow blue plates, off-colour Niagara Glass Factory decanters, have been helter-skeltered on new bric-a-brac around the walls." Doubtless she meant brackets.

Almost simultaneously, diners at two tables rise to leave. The tallest man from one group looks back at six plates of charred toast, untouched, cut in neat triangles, fanned out like a flamenco dancer's accoutrements, garnished with pinky-red radish roses.

Rita, now the only customer in the room, has two hours to kill. She might kill the friend and erstwhile chauffeur who has parked her here. "Look Ri," Roxanne had insisted, "We aren't both going to deify the place. Stay here while I check out the real estate in the neighbouring burg. It'll give you plenty of time to fricassee the food or scribble your raptures. Don't budge or you'll get chomped by those nasty blackflies and snaggle-toothed beavers."

How could she know that she had abandoned Rita to an eatery sans kitchen— just a microwave oven on a serving counter, can opener below. A beaver, properly sautéed in a few onions minces might not be so bad at this point.

Rita wishes she could go somewhere else, somewhere where the air conditioning is not on full blast, where four and twenty MacIntosh apples are bursting through pies, freshly caught perch are being poached, fiddleheads fiddled with, maple tarts sugared. But her ex-husband—may he rest in peace wherever criminal lawyers who cheat on their wives and leave them penniless are buried, often quipped—to her friends and his—that he was married to the only woman who stepped out her front door and couldn't find the garage. If she leaves, Rita knows she'll vanish.

Jennifer, lipstick freshly applied, has left. Behind the counter, Stephanie totals the day's receipts and expenses. 2 tuna olive spinach wraps, 4 macadamia nut cookies, 2 hot chocolates, 9 expresso-type coffees, 6 tea and toasts, 1 kiwi chutney sardine spinach wrap $102.68 IN, $167.00 OUT "Save something for tax installments Steph." "Yah dad, sure." Eight hours standing in the restaurant for eight months. She aches all over. If Russell ever shows up after their last big fight, he can massage her back right there on table number five. That should draw a crowd! Maybe her high school guidance counselor knew something after all. "You're a very creative person Stephanie. Be a hairdresser or a manicurist. Your kid brother can take over your grandfather's business. He's got the brains for it!" Stephanie wishes the old biddy in the stuffy red sweater—Christ, it's the middle of July!—would go home. She wishes she could go home.

Stephanie wants to wash her hair. And then, she wants to cry.

For Rita, there is suddenly a pop of champagne! This juicy review could be her year's supply of Norwegian caviar, her return to her rightful place setting. Gourmand readers savour the tang of acid ink. True Blue Restaurant is almost too good to be true. "With little else to choose from, I had ordered the kiwi chutney shrimp spinach wrap. This is Canada eh? But allow me to embellish. The presentation was divine, a celestial sphere of kiwi, half-moons of shrimp, a constellation of spinach wrap spun against a heavenly blue charger, the signs of the Zodiac in parsley and pimento, in perfect harmony. But, but—the kiwi fruit rivaled the smallest and oldest bite from Eve's apple, the shrimp mere parings from Oliver Twist's begging bowl, the parsley limp (from fright?)

while the green spinach wrap was as turgid and unyielding as the sarcophagus of an impoverished Egyptian princess." Rita exhales. Is she going too far? She watches the girl behind the counter. Stephanie is far too young for the faded brown chignon uncurling at the back of her neck like an undercooked brioche en couronne. Probably the same age as her daughter. If she had one.

The power of words! Her words! She could concoct a completely different review. The sarcophagus wrap could be fairy-godmothered to an anise scented floating garden of prime western verdure, the shrimp an import from the usually inaccessible waters of the Royal House of St. Simeon's and so on. Of course she couldn't risk publication in Gourmand, but Ontario Epicure, well, she could use her old pseudonym; they'd claw even for that.

She looks again at the young woman behind the counter. Thirty-five minutes to closing and Roxanne's return. A great review for True Blue and then what? The restaurant becoming a swinging door with hundreds racing in and soon running out. No. A girl who garnishes burnt toast should not be running a restaurant, at least not yet and certainly not without a stove, maybe, not ever, but certainly with a little guidance and a lot of warning. This might be Historic True Blue but most restaurants were heartbreak house. Rita saw them open and she saw them close, chefs kill and be killed, investors leap from tall buildings, a fickle public applauds, then forage elsewhere.

She motions to Stephanie. "Sweetie, only a few minutes before closing. You look exhausted! How would you like me to buy you a cup of chamomile? I can see that you love decorating food. It certainly is pretty. We might have a lot to talk about."

For the first time that day, maybe that month, Stephanie smiles. She guesses the lady in the red sweater at table number three is old enough to be her grandmother, always cold, poor thing. She fills two mugs with water and places them in the microwave, moves towards the lady at table three.

"And sweetie," Rita calls, "bring a batch of those cookies over here as well. It looks like those macadamias have gotten cosy with some pretty grand white chocolate chunks.

# The Mezuzah

*Fiona Gold Kroll*

I spent my last night at home in the darkened cellar cuddled up to Maman. When dawn broke, she locked the blue wooden door, carefully removed the Mezuzah. She wrapped it in a handkerchief and slipped it into her pocket before we peddled our bicycles away from the distant crackle of gunfire.

Maman changed after Papa disappeared. Her plump cheeks sunk, her nails chewed down to the quick, and her worn out clothes hung on her like potato sacks. Frequently ill-tempered, she seldom smiled.

"Stay close to me, Camille."

Maman's anxious face crumpled in furrows that appeared deeper as each day passed.

I was afraid.

"Where are we going?" I asked.

"Le Chambon-sur-Lignon, we'll be safe there." "And Papa?"

Maman turned her head away. I stared at her blankly. Why did she ignore me when I asked about Papa?

We rode along the dirt road beside clumps of grass that dripped with beads of water from the early morning dew. The sun rose and cars passed us with people squeezed inside and heavy suitcases tied to the roof as they laboured on their journey to the unknown, trailed by clouds of dust. The August heat burned through the sleeves of my cotton dress. It hadn't rained in days and my fingernails were already caked with grime.

Maman pointed to a village just off the road.

"I need some water," she called out to me.

Wind whipped my hair around my head when I leaned into the corner and peddled my bike down the dirt road into the main square. I passed a stray dog barking and a goat tied to a tree, bleating. It was a town without people, only the empty crusts of homes, smashed doors, walls pitted with bullet holes and chunks of blown out glass scattered across the cobblestone roads. Maman wiped beads of sweat from her forehead on the sleeve of her blouse. She didn't see the heap of bricks on the ground and when she rounded the corner her front tire clipped the edge of the pile, and she flew over the handle bars landing head first into the rubble.

"Maman!" I cried.

I tossed my bike to the ground. Blood oozed from a deep gash on the top of her head. Scared, I looked around for help. A grey haired man with a ruddy face, mustache and a large belly hurried towards us. He stooped down and examined the cut. Maman winced.

"It's alright. Let me help you." His voice was comforting.

The man raised Maman to her feet and led her to the only home in the village with windows and doors.

"Sit," he said.

He filled a bowl with water, ripped a white sheet into strips, cleaned the gash and secured the dressing under her chin. Maman looked ashen, her skin transparent.

He offered us a bowl of soup, thick with carrots and potatoes and in spite of the heat outside I savoured every drop.

"Where are you going?" he asked.

Maman hesitated.

"Le Puy, do you know it?"

"Of course, but it's at least seventy-five kilometers from here. Why don't you rest and spend the night? You can sleep in the barn."

Maman hesitated and locked her large sunken eyes on mine. I could sense she didn't trust the man.

"Thank you. You have been most kind Monsieur but I feel much better. We will continue on."

He protested, but Maman shook his hand and we left.

"Maman, why did you tell him we are going to Le Puy?"

"Only a collaborator would stay in an empty, bombed out village and have enough vegetables to make a thick soup. I couldn't tell him where we are really going, he could turn us over to the Nazis."

I knew what that could mean. I thought back to when our neighbors the Potanskis, were arrested in the middle of the night. I heard the screech of tires when the SS pulled up in front of their house and kicked open the door; the snarling dogs, gun shots and cries as they forced Sara and her parents into a truck and drove away.

We got back on our bikes and disappeared down the road towards the river Lignon du Velay; past lush green fields and more villages broken by war. Exhausted, tears rolled down my cheeks.

"Maman, I can't go on. I'm hot and tired."

"Come, we'll rest under a tree beside the river."

Maman helped me off my bike, wiped my face with the palms of her hands, held me tight and kissed the top of my head. She had not done that in a long time and I let my body sink into the safety of her arms. Together, we walked down to the river where I rinsed my hands and dunked my head into the cool water. When will this nightmare be over?

It was dark by the time we reached Le Chambon-sur-Lignon and my entire body hurt. We rode our bicycles down the narrow cobblestone road towards a small bridge, leaned them up against the railing and sat down to rest on the blankets we brought with us. Exhausted, Maman held her head in her hands and looked down, I rubbed my eyes and when I opened them, I saw a man with a dark beard and beret walk towards us.

Maman stood up.

"Rachel Goldberg?" "Yes," replied Mama.

"Follow me, my name is Henri." As we trailed Henri across the narrow street, Maman explained how the Resistance arranged for us to find refuge with the Chambonais who would also help us cross the border.

"And Papa?"

Maman stopped, turned to me and held my hands.

"I can't tell you Camille, but I promise we'll all be together soon."

We spent the next three nights resting in a safe house in Le Chambon. I will never forget the kindness of strangers. They handed us false papers before we began the 300-kilometer trek to the Swiss border. We had assumed names and I wondered if I would ever be known as Camille Goldberg again. Sometimes we traveled between haystacks on a horse drawn wagon, and sometimes we walked, always at night and in the company of two guides who disappeared into the forest when we reached the border.

We were completely alone. My heart pounded with fear. "Documents," said the guard.

He looked at each of us and carefully examined our papers. Every minute that passed felt like an hour. Freedom was merely steps away. I could see it; I could almost touch it. Finally, he lifted the gate and waved us on. Maman tucked our papers into her pocket and together we entered Switzerland.

"Papa?" I whispered.

"Keep walking," Maman said.

And, as we reached the edge of the tree line, a familiar figure stepped out from behind a large fir tree.

"Papa! Papa!" I yelled.

I ran into his arms while Maman walked towards him, tears rolling down her cheeks. Papa explained to me how weeks earlier, he made his way to Le Chambon and arranged for Maman and me to meet him in Switzerland. We stood gathered in a bundle; touched, kissed and held each other until the tears gave way to laughter and we walked hand in hand into our new life.

When the war ended, we immigrated to America. After Maman died, I sorted through her little black lacquer keepsake box and when I raised the lid, there was the Mezuzah from our home and the bandage that wrapped her head the day she fell from her bicycle in France so many years ago. How could I ever forget?

# A Boundless Journey

*Sam Hoffer*

This was Pierre's first trip with his parents to Honfleur, where his father had often come with his family when he was a boy. Pierre's grandparents had died before he was born, but his father kept their memory and his own enchantment with Honfleur alive in the bedtime stories that he told his son.

Today, as he and his parents walked among the ancient buildings that he had heard so much about, Pierre could almost hear the clip clop sounds of horses pulling wagons in the cobbled streets. He imagined crowds of people just as now, eagerly making their way to the banks of the river that coursed through the town.

Pierre held his mother's hand as they strolled along. Then, rounding a corner, they came upon a breathtaking view of the river, glistening white sailboats moored at its sides. The adjoining sidewalks were bounded by tall, narrow buildings, spots of painted curtains visible in their windows and brilliant awnings sheltering the crowded streets.

He was the first to see it, commanding a grassy knoll at the end of the walkway. He pulled his hand free and ran toward it, but stopped suddenly, dazzled by the beauty of the carousel. He had never seen such a wonder. The outside of the massive crown was adorned with mirrored shields that spoke of mysteries and haunted dreams. The shields were separated by gigantic diamonds that must have been stolen by murderous pirates from the treasure chests of kings. A gold ceiling adorned the enormous wheel. In it were embedded paintings of swordsmen in the throes of battle with daunting foes; others, portrayed warriors bounding off on horseback, the conquest of a maiden in their arms, their victory celebrated by a sea of lights.

Beneath these images he saw scores of horses thundering toward him. He leapt onto the fiercest stallion, narrowly avoiding a deadly spill into a gaping chasm. He charged fearlessly across the void, galloping into the wind, pursued by legions of loyal soldiers.

# Still A Prisoner

*Gerda Frieberg*

A spool of thread lay on the floor in the corner of the mill. I picked it up and wrapped the yarn around my fingers. I looked around the vast space, and the memory of working for hours under the scowl of the SS came flooding back; a frightened child, a slave labourer.

I was unsure if I wanted to return to the camp when I received a message from journalist Marisa Fox-Bevilacqua. Marisa committed herself to honour the memory of her mother, one of 5,000 Jewish girls, the forgotten victims of Ober-Alstadt, and other sub camps of Gross Rosen in then Czechoslovakia. On May 9, 2016, a monument in memory of the Female Slave Labourers was to be unveiled. As a journalist, Marisa embarked on creating a documentary that will shed new light on women's suffering. Years after the end of the Second World War, she searched for survivor witnesses. By now only those girls who were 14 to 16 years old when they arrived in the camps are living. I am one of those survivors.

On April 1942 at the age of 16 I arrived in Ober-Altstadt, confused and frightened. A group of girls were led to the Ignatz spinning mill. The machine I was assigned to had 120 spools. The yarn easily broke when it transferred to large spools. My job was to rejoin it because each spool had to contain equal yardage. If it was less, we were accused of sabotage. We knew what that meant: we were replaceable.

We were housed on the upper floor of an adjacent building of the factory. A few months later more girls arrived and barracks were built at the edge of the river escarpment. Each morning, before leaving for work we lined up, we were counted and marched to the factory with a piece of bread, our food ration for the day. On returning from work, we again lined up and were counted.

As the ghettos across Europe were liquidated, more girls arrived at the camp, by then taken over by the SS and designated as a concentration camp. Major changes were made. Barbed wire now surrounded the camp and the SS took over day to day operations. We were stripped naked, and given a number. We no longer had a name, all our belongings were confiscated. We were perpetually hungry, covered with lice, in fear of getting sick and frightened of beatings. It was a time when it was easier to die than to live. We prayed to see another sunset, our strength slipping.

There were less supplies arriving at the factory, which meant we were no longer needed. In late April 1945, instead of going to the mill, we were marched outside the local town of Trutnov, given shovels and instructed to dig a ditch around the town. It was to prevent the enemy's tanks from entering. We were warned that if we didn't finish in time we would be shot.

We returned to the camp exhausted and full of fear. Scared, we stood outside to be counted. When the SS commander finished the count, he faced us and said, "You might think that the war is coming to and end, but I want you to know that you will never leave this place alive. The camp is rigged with dynamite. We will blow you up before we leave."

We returned to the barracks; no one spoke. Three long years, 1,123 days of hell on earth. Only a stubborn will to live through horror kept us alive. We came so close; our hope, our dreams of freedom shattered.

Morning came. I stood at the window. There were no shouts from the guards. Their barracks seemed empty. How much time did we have left? Suddenly, I heard the heavy thud of military footsteps. This is the end. I look and realize the soldiers are not wearing Nazi uniforms. They were South African prisoners of war, who were held in a camp near the town. They marched to the gate, and cut the barbed wire.

"Girls, the war is over," they yelled. Our prayers were answered.

They told us the Czech partisans were watching the camp for days. During the night they disabled the mines and saved our lives. A few Czech women left us bread and walked away. We didn't have an opportunity to thank them, but we will always remember their deeds.

It was May 9, 1945, we stood outside the camp gate, Germany defeated. Our dream to survive became reality. Children who become adults, no family, no education, no home and no country that welcomed us.

Today and in years to come, 5,000 girls wearing invisible tattoos, the forgotten victims will now be remembered. The memorial erected will remain as a warning to future generations. It is our sacred obligation to remember the victims and honour the survivors. On that day our bodies were liberated.

I let go of the thread knotted tight around my fingers and walked away from the mill. The survivors will be free when they will be laid to rest.

# Matzo Balls

*Jenny Roger*

Every family has their own way of making Matzo balls, whether they are large or small, hard or soft.

My family has a very special tradition.

My great-grandmother came to Canada at the turn of the twentieth century. She cooked the type of food she learned from her mother in Lithuania.

I always thought that my grandmother had a quirky family recipe for Matzo Balls, but recently I found out that it is a Lithuanian (Litvak) recipe steeped in tradition and mysticism.

My Great-grandmother Raizie made her Matzo Balls with a filling in the center that consisted of Matzo Ball batter with cinnamon added to it. The filling was called the Neshama, which meant soul in Hebrew and Yiddish.

I was told by my mother that Raizie loved cinnamon so much, that was why she used it in her Matzah Balls.

This is the only Matzo Ball recipe I know of that has a Neshama.

Today it is a trend for younger Jewish cooks to stuff Matzo Balls with mushrooms, chopped parsley, sweet potatoes, cooked onions, whatever they can come up with, but they call it stuffing, not Neshama.

Matzo Balls are one of the great foods of Ashkenazi, Eastern European cuisine, dating back to the Medieval Ages. They were a perfect food to add to a soup during Passover, when the Passover dietary restrictions made it very difficult for the Jewish cook.

Originally known as Knaidel they were made of crumbled matzo meal, eggs and spices. The late Gil Marks tells us in his Encyclopedia of Jewish Food that the first recipe in English for Matzah Balls comes from The Jewish Manual (London, 1846). The recipe's seasonings were "a little pepper, salt, ginger, and nutmeg."

Imagine how much work it took to grind by hand the matzo into a meal. It was only in the early twentieth century in New York after Manischewitz created a Matzo grinder and started selling packaged Matzo Meal that it became easier for the home cook to make Matzo Balls.

I'm sure my great grandmother used matzo meal; I know my grandmother and mother did.   But where did the Neshama come from?

I found the answer from American food writer and Jewish culinary expert Joan Nathan.

She had discovered recipes with Neshama from South African Jewish cookbooks of Litvak (Lithuanian) descent. The Litvaks arrived in South Africa in the late 18th century, and kept their food traditions longer than American Jews did.

Coming to Canada, Raizie also kept her East European and Litvak food traditions; there was no "melting pot" for her to melt into.

Doing her own research into the matter Joan Nathan discussed the Neshama with Israeli professor of Folklore at Hebrew University, Dov Noy.

He told Joan that the cinnamon is crucial:

"It is like the secret sweetness within the spice box at the Havdalah service that ends the Sabbath," he said. "The cinnamon stuffing represents a wish to stretch the sweetness of the Sabbath meal (or Seder meal) for as long as possible."

This is how my family recipe turned from being quirky into something beautiful and mystical.  This is how my mother handed it down to me:

*Matzo Balls with Neshama*
Save fat from soup (not scum) which should be about ½ - ¾ cup liquid. (May take 2 days for this amount of fat to form). Beat this liquid into 2 eggs and 2 egg whites. Add salt, then gradually stir in matzo meal until thick.

*Neshama*
2 egg yolks
Heaping tablespoon schmaltz
Salt
Cinnamon
Heaping tablespoon matzo meal

Stir these ingredients together.
Allow both mixtures to stand in refrigerator for at least 2 hours. Make kneidlach one half hour before eating. Boil pot of salted water. Wet hands, put some of kneidlach mixture on hand, then add about a teaspoon of Neshama mixture in the middle. Wrap kneidlach around this Neshama, and drop in the boiling water. Cook for ½ an hour.

*Matzo Balls (My Version)*
My husband's parents came from Germany, and as German Jews, they did not speak Yiddish. I always called my Matzo Balls Kneidlach, and he called them Knuedel. We didn't know what the other person was talking about until our first Passover together when I made Kneidlach he said: "that's what I'm talking about, those are Knuedel." Since then we refer to them as Matzo Balls.

Both my husband and I don't really like the Neshama so I make mine without. My recipe is based on Lillian Kaplan's, who taught cooking to Toronto women in the 1960's.

I like to make my Matzo Balls medium sized, and soft and fluffy. My mother-in-law made hers small and hard.

The secret for fluffy Matzo Balls is to really beat up the eggs until they are foamy before you add the other ingredients. You also cannot skip refrigerating the batter, it is needed so the balls will hold together and not disintegrate in the boiling water.

The reason why you cook the matzo balls in a pot of water, and not in the chicken soup is so they don't absorb the chicken soup. They taste lighter cooked in salted water. If there are leftover cooked matzo balls, then I add them to the soup to be reheated.

*Matzo Balls:*
Ingredients:
2 extra large eggs
2 tablespoons water
1 teaspoon salt
½ cup plus 1 tablespoon matzo meal
2 tablespoons margarine or chicken fat

Beat the eggs in a bowl until they are combined and add the water and salt. Beat well until foamy. Add matzo meal, margarine or chicken fat and combine. Cover the bowl and put in refrigerator for at least one hour until the batter firms up.

To make:
Boil a large pot of water and add salt. Shape the batter into balls in your hand and drop into the boiling water. The

size of the balls depends on how large you want your matzo balls to be. Reduce the water to a simmer, cover the pot and cook for about 45 minutes to one hour. The cooked matzo balls are ready to be added to your hot soup.

# Paris City of Lights

*Raizie Jacobson*

Friday night city of darkness
Black, Black
Black boots, black pants, black shirt, black mask
Pow, pow, pause, rat-a-tat-tat, pause, pow, pow
Screams, tears, fear
Bodies, pools of blood,
Survivors, bystanders,
Vacant eyes, shock, sadness, depression, disbelief
Lives changed forever

# How Did This Dog Happen?

*Sam Hoffer*

It snuck up gradually, like the creeping realization of some fundamental truth that won't be denied and then it burst upon us. It happened in the morning when I take Rachel to the subway, the start of her daily trip to work. A time when we chat about random things or try to squeeze in an important piece of business that we forgot to deal with the night before.

"I hate this darkness," I grumble as we weave around the snow banks. "Months of it and it's going to get worse." Rachel doesn't bother to answer. I know that she agrees.

"I think we need a dog," Rachel says, almost to herself. But I hear her and it registers. I wonder at how evenly I take it. Almost as if I had said it myself. And instantly, I just know that our lives have changed. Forever.

I don't ask her why. I can feel it in my bones – an idea whose time has come. Could it be because she thinks I'm getting bored at home, in my retirement? Or that our kids, though in their twenties, could use a buddy? Or, could it be the constant refrain of friends talking about their grandchildren?

"It would be good for the kids," I offer, just as a red light begins to flash in the corner of my mind.

"But who is going to take care of it?" I ask, my heart suddenly searching for an exit from my chest. "I sure don't want to be the one going out in the snow and sleet to walk the dog at five in the morning all winter."

Rachel knows me too well. That evening we go on line, make some phone calls the next morning and, three peaceful months later, we pick up a brand new Havanese puppy whose name was destined by the stars to be – Rusty.

It's now been a month since Rusty's arrival. My kids have regressed to ages five or six and Rachel has re-discovered a voice I haven't heard since Michael and Esther were babies. What is clearly one of the simplest names in the English language has become an entire high-pitched sentence: Russ…Teee?!"

The sound is riveting. My ears perk up at the same time as Rusty's. Is something wrong? Whatever it is, I let Rusty go first. And it works. By the time I show up, Rachel says, as if she's almost forgotten that I live here, "Oh, there you are. I was going to tell you something, but I've forgotten what…"

The notion that I'm entirely dispensable has become contagious. They all arrive sooner or later - Rachel and Esther from work and Michael, who has discovered that there is day after night, from his room. All I'm now good for is to answer the only question they seem capable of asking, "Where's Rusty?"

They've all left now. Rusty and I are alone. I've fed him and like a hovering hawk I'm watching, watching until, with equal portions of amazement and disbelief, I see it: the telltale twist of his body, the eyes searching for a private spot. As if my life depends on it, I make a dash for him, scoop him up in one hand while struggling to maneuver my arm into a coat sleeve with the other. My hat is gripped firmly between my teeth and I'm praying that my gloves are in my pocket. Oh, and I need a bag!

Desperately, I drop my hat and prepare to pick up the plastic poop bag with my teeth. I stare at it. I know it's never been used, but I just can't bring myself to do it. Rusty is squirming, trying to break free. Frantically, I slide the glass doors open and am about to step outside. I'm in my socks!

Just then the phone rings. Instinctively, I push the speaker button, immediately regretting what I've done.

"How's Rusty?" Rachel asks buoyantly.

"Fine!" I shout, while with a sweeping motion that would rival the best of Baryshnikov, I offer Rusty to the snow-covered steps. "I'm just putting him outside to do his business and I'll call you right back."

"Oh, Ok!" she replies, the glee in her voice palpable. "Let me know what happens!"

In the evening, not long after dinner, my eyelids droop and my body draws me to the couch for a nap. I couldn't be happier. Rusty, dozing on Rachel's lap peers through the mane of hair covering his eyes to see where I am going. The ringer on the phone is off and the lights on the front porch are out. Only an earthquake can get me now.

On the edge of sleep, I feel that deep contentment that tells me that I'm as near to unconsciousness as you can get. Purest nirvana... and, ... and, an unmistakable sensation that something is snuggling up against me, burrowing its way relentlessly toward my head. I resist the thought, willing it away into my dreams. Not a chance. It's getting closer and then, with an explosive burst of energy it erupts, a fierce nose in my face and a slobbering lick across my mouth.

My hand shoots up and my eyes squeeze shut in a vain attempt at self-defence. Somewhere in the dark recesses of my mind, in the hazy remnants of my shattered sleep, a question begins to form: how did this happen? I can't fathom an answer. I don't remember a thing. Until, a moment later, when I hear that inimitable, loving call, "Russ...Teee?!"

# Hotel Fire

*Carol Green*

I first got to know my future husband, Ian, on a weeklong school trip to London, England. I was seventeen and it was 1972. Little did we know that the trip would be memorable for other reasons too! Several high schools in the Toronto area joined together, including Ian's school. By the time we began the trip, there were kids from all over, including me from Ottawa. Ian's parents were friends with my cousin's parents, who were chaperones on the trip, so we convinced our parents that little could go wrong with familiar adults on board.

Of course, many things went wrong, such as my cousin and I missing events and showing up late, often rushing out of a London cab after missing the tour bus. We were also busted for smoking and drinking in the hotel lobby bar, as well as charging our sickly sweet Singapore Slings to Ian's parents' hotel bill, for reasons unknown to me now. As the bar entryway was partially obscured, we did not think that anyone could see us sitting in there before dinner each night. Ian told me that his Mom would walk by and say to his Dad, "There are those idiots again." But they never mentioned the bar tab or the smoking to us or our parents, bless them. They understood teenage behavior.

At the hotel, my cousin and I occupied a basement suite with several girls. Our bedroom was straight out of Oliver Twist. It had a black metal fence above a deep window well from which we viewed the street. Indeed, early one foggy evening, I commented that a man walking by looked eerily like the character, Fagin, with his thin face, hawk nose, beard and raggedy overcoat and gloves.

Nothing life threatening happened on the trip until the night of the hotel fire. For once, our annoying behavior was a blessing. I am sure our roommates were utterly fed up with our antics, as we chattered about something or other at 2 a.m. one night. Suddenly, we both smelled smoke. My cousin bounded over our twin beds and touched the door handle. It was hot, so we woke the other girls right away.

We yelled "Fire" in our biggest voices, threw open the giant window panes, and scrambled up and over the metal fence. We had to stop one of our roommates from repeatedly returning to our room to get her things. My cousin slapped her to bring her to her senses, terrified she could lose her life. Then we ran to the hotel lobby to notify them about the fire.

I guess our earlier noise had aroused quite a few people, as many were now streaming outside, all of us in our bedclothes. A man, woken from the commotion nearby, bicycled up and gave my cousin and me an old pea coat and a blanket. He said he was keeping the things for the "rag-and-bone man" but with the sound of the hotel being evacuated, he felt we needed them more. He was very kind.

Of course, the fire engines came up. We searched for and found Ian, his sister, and his parents. BBC TV came up and interviewed Ian's dad, though he refused to give his name, so he was on the telly and in the newspaper as "an unidentified American." I still have the newspaper.

Luckily, no one was seriously hurt or killed in this fire. None of us realized that this was the same hotel where eleven Canadians, including high school students, died in a fire the previous year. I recall reading the horrifying story in The Ottawa Journal about a girl who jumped from her balcony and died. The hotel had in the past year changed its name, which tricked the school, but the tour company ought to have caught it.

The following year after our visit, there was another arson attack; this time the arsonist was caught, the same man who had set the other fires. The fire was timed for March Break when Canadian students were staying there. It turned out he had an axe to grind with a Canadian ex-girlfriend. He took out his anger on innocent Canadians, many of them children. I hope he is never let out of prison.

In the meantime, we learned that the fire that was set during our stay at the hotel began just outside our door. A mattress had been doused with a flammable liquid. It burned the hallway. Several rooms, including ours, had smoke damage. Our clothes reeked of smoke for the rest of the trip. The tour company was supposed to notify our parents in Canada that we were all OK. My parents only learned of the fire after we returned safely to Canadian soil.

Ian, and I, along with his sister and my cousin, share this experience. Ian also met his best buddy on this trip. We are all connected for life through many shared adventures, including the hotel fire. Ian and I were married twenty-five years after the fire. When many of us reunited in 2015 for my 60th birthday celebration, it was great to reminisce about old times. None of us will ever forget the London hotel fire. It is part of the history that brought us together so many years ago.

# When a Daughter Leaves the Shtetl

*Fiona Gold Kroll*

In 1908 Sheva embarks on the most important journey of her life.

She crosses the cobblestone street and cuts through the village square on her way to Rivka's house. It's spring; green leaves unfold from sticky brown buds on trees and yellow daffodils mingle with blades of grass, bowing to one another in the gentle breeze. It looks peaceful enough until a black cloud appears in the sky like the pogroms that send Jews fleeing in fear when thugs shatter windows and ransack homes. Just after Yankel's birth Moshe decides the family must leave the shtetl and make their way to England.

Moshe makes the voyage first, obtains employment, sets up a home and eventually sends Sheva the money to purchase a ticket to join him. After three long years of separation, Sheva counts the days until they are together again.

Sheva and Rivka grew up together; laughed and cried together and today while sipping hot tea in the shtetl, they reminisce about childhood adventures. The clock on the mantel ticks in the background. Sheva glances at the time, stands up, brushes off her long skirt and drapes her shawl around her shoulders.

"Rivka, I could spend hours talking, but I must go, I have to pack. Promise me you'll write?"

"I will—I promise."

They hug each other so tight that Sheva can barely breathe. She kisses Rivka's tear stained cheeks.

"Look after Lazer and the children," Sheva says.

She holds out her hand to Yankel.

"Come Tatala, let's go home."

Together, they walk past the little wood frame shul where Sheva davens upstairs on Shabbat with the other women. She pokes her head in the shop next door and says good-bye to Motel the butcher. Not that his meat was ever good. Once Sheva marched into his store and slapped a piece of cooked brisket on the counter.

"You call this a piece of meat, Motel? It's tough like leather!" Tiny, fearless Sheva is no pushover.

She walks around the corner, down the gravel road, past the well. Yankel kicks pebbles into the ditch, just as Sheva did as a child. In the distance she sees her father, sitting outside the house on his old wooden chair. Face drawn and pale, he strokes his red beard and pushes his black kippah back and forth on his head. Yankel runs ahead, and climbs on his Zaideh's lap.

"Tatti, are you alright?" says Sheva.

Her father wraps his arms around Yankel and kisses his cheeks.

"I wish you would leave him here with Mameh and me. You're going to live in an unknown world. Will he study Torah; will he attend Yeshiva?"

"Tatti, Yankel is my son. I could never leave without him. I don't know what the future holds, but you have my word, Moshe and I will raise our children as honest Jews."

Just then, her mother steps outside.

"So, did you ask her?" she says.

"Mameh—how could you even imagine I would leave Yankel behind?"

"Shush, let's not argue. The soup is hot, the bread warm. Come inside and eat before the food gets cold," says her mother.

Sheva sits down and looks around the table at her brothers and sisters and wonders if she will see them again. Maybe they'll come to England; life is full of maybes, she thinks.

After she tucks Yankel into bed, Sheva folds the few clothes she is taking with her and puts them on top of the dresser. Tired from the emotion of the day, she lies on the bed beside her son and pulls the feather comforter over the two of them. Her eyes close and she tries to imagine her Moshe. She reaches out to touch his face; soon we'll be together again. Yankel sighs when Sheva pulls him into her. She strokes his hair, and kisses his forehead before her head sinks into the pillow.

Sheva wakes with a start. Paper burns, kindling crackles as her father stokes the wood stove. She gets up and pulls the lace curtain back from the window. It is still dark outside. She splashes water on her face. Yankel stirs and rubs his eyes; she washes his hands and face and helps him dress. Half asleep, neither one of them can eat, it's too early.

"At least have a hot drink," her mother says, throwing her hands in the air in frustration.

Sheva lays their clothes in a clean linen sheet with two loaves of bread for the journey and ties the ends together in a bundle. She buttons up Yankel's coat and wraps herself in a shawl.

"Have you got all your tickets?"

"Yes, Tatti I do," she smiles.

She closes the old door to the house and rubs her fingers over dents and cracks in the wood; several are from age, others from the hoodlums who beat down the door, just to scare them from time to time. Tatti turns the key; the lock clicks. Sheva knows she will never return.

In the early morning darkness, the four of them walk to the train station in silence.

They sit down on the bench beside the tracks; Yankel yawns and snuggles with his grandfather. Slowly dawn breaks, birds chirp and the rising sun brightens the sky with pink and mauve shadows chasing night clouds over the horizon.

Suddenly the quiet is broken by a harsh whistle. A black engine rumbles down the tracks, spewing white smoke from its funnel like an angry bull. Yankel buries his head in Sheva's lap and covers his ears. The train clatters into the station, and stops with a hiss of steam and screeching brakes.

Sheva hugs her mother.

"Good-bye Mameh. Take care of yourself and make sure everyone helps you next Pesach."

She turns to her father and looks into his blue eyes, moist with sadness. Her beloved Tatti the most wonderful father, she could hope for; pious, patient, kind and caring.

"Look after you and Mameh," she says with tears rolling down her face.

He hugs her tight and kisses her forehead. "Go, be well, all of you."

She takes Yankel's hand and climbs on the train. They sit by a window and when the train begins its slow chug out of the station, Yankel stands on his seat and waves good-bye to his Bubba and Zaideh.

They travel all day, stopping in Vienna at night. Sheva knows the two loaves of bread will not be enough to feed them for the entire journey, so they spend the night at the Jewish shelter, where they eat and rest. In the morning, they board a train to Bremen, and finally embark on the ship. It takes two nights to cross the wild North Sea with only one loaf of bread to eat that Sheva carries with her. She sings songs, tells Yankel stories in Yiddish and cradles him in her arms until they both fall into an exhausted sleep.

Moshe paces on the wharf waiting for Sheva and Yankel to disembark at the London docks. His anxious eyes search faces on the crowded deck. Then he sees them walking down the gangway and when they reach the bottom, he scoops up Yankel in his arms and hugs and kisses Sheva. She removes her head scarf and runs her hand through the soft waves in her hair.

"Where's your sheitel?" he asks.

"I don't remember."

Sheva tilts her face to the clear blue sky and soaks up the warmth from the sun. She looks at Moshe, smiles and together my grandparents and uncle walk hand in hand with hope for a better life in England.

# Our Picture

*Carol Green*

My husband and I were married late in life, at the age of forty-two. Six weeks after our 1997 wedding, my Aunt and Uncle hosted Thanksgiving at the ancestral home of my late grandparents, where my mom and her sister lived as children. I spent many summers there in my early childhood. I knew the house well.

My Aunt and Uncle had been lovingly restoring the big white heritage house on the main street of Quyon, Québec for many years. As part of the restoration process, many articles were left in the identical positions they had occupied for decades.

In my late grandparents' bedroom, there had always hung a charming picture of a mature couple with their new baby. The picture was dated 1931 and had been an illustration in a popular magazine of the day that had been cut out and framed. I had always loved this picture, as had my Grandmother. The expressions on the parents' faces are radiant as they gaze upon their child. The boy lies upon a white pillow encircled with lace and tied with a large light blue satin bow.

While we were guests at this Thanksgiving celebration, we were assigned my grandparents' bedroom. Just before my husband and I left for home the next day, I considered asking my aunt if I could possibly take the picture of the couple with the new baby. I don't know why, but something stopped me from pursuing this question with her. I felt somewhere in my bones that the picture was unnecessary. I did not ask Grace for the picture.

Shortly after we returned to Toronto, I found out I was pregnant. I gave birth to our son, on June 10, 1998. He is our miracle. It became clear why my grandmother had found the picture so alluring, and why I had not needed to have it. We WERE the couple in the picture.

# Burned Money

*Gerda Frieberg*

I lived with my parents and sister in Bielszowice, a town in what was then Upper Silesia when WWII began and Germany invaded Poland on September 1, 1939. My parents ran a successful business, and my father was a respected member of the community who received a medal of bravery after he served in the German army during WWI. But as Jews, we no longer had rights to own a business, go to school or wear medals.

By the middle of October, terrible news reached us. The governing Nazi authority decided to make the area we lived in Judenrein (free of Jews). They began by removing all men from age 16 to age 65. Father told me that he would have to leave and in October, police arrived at our door with an order to pick him up.

Days and weeks went by after they took my father away. No one knew what had happened to the men since October. Mother was constantly in touch with friends in neighbouring towns. I didn't leave her side because of her anxiety attacks. The Nazis had confiscated all valuables from the Jews, and we had no source of income.

Fortunately, she did have German money, since we travelled a lot in Germany. This would be sufficient for groceries. But, she feared that the Nazis could come any day and search our home and find it, so she decided to hide it.

The logical place where they might not look, was the baking oven, since no one was baking cakes in these troubled times. She placed the banknotes in a box, put it in the oven, and covered it with kindling and coal.

Weeks went by, and one day a letter arrived. On a closer look we noticed that it had a Russian postage stamp. We opened the letter and recognized Father's handwriting. He had escaped while others were being shot; hid for two days and walked through a forest until he reached a village unaware that he had crossed the border into Russia. He had Jewish friends who welcomed him into their home and found work. He missed us terribly and eagerly awaited letters from home.

We were overjoyed to learn that Father was alive and safe. Mother decided to bake a cake to celebrate the good news. She lit a fire in the oven and prepared the batter, when suddenly to her horror, she remembered that she had hidden the money under the coal. She doused the fire with water and pulled out the charred box. What now? We were penniless and had no money to buy a piece of bread.

A few days went by, then, in desperation, she came up with a bold idea. She carefully wrapped the box and mailed it with an explanatory letter to the Deutsche Reichsbank in Berlin. She explained that there had been a fire in our home and that we had lost everything but were able to retrieve the burned money. Would it be possible to identify the numbers and replace it? She signed the letter, "Elfriede Steinitz." Would "Chutzpah" be the proper word? The only hope was that the bank would not identify her name as Jewish. Well, they did not, and a week later, new crisp bills arrived. This was indeed cause for celebration.

# The Kettle

*Jenny Roger*

A quiet sigh involuntarily passed my lips as I sat down.

"Oy Vey Iz Mir," I cried as I realized how bone weary I was.

I sat down to enjoy a cup of tea in peace and quiet. The two oldest boys 14 and 16 years old were at work, the rest of the children at school and the baby sleeping. My husband was at his tiny shoe repair shop, hopefully earning some money, not just wasting his time gossiping with the good for nothings who like to hang around his shop and chatter all day.

The sun shone brightly on this cold fall afternoon. I had sneaked in a precious extra piece of coal into the stove to warm the kitchen up. We had just finished celebrating the High Holidays. How time was flying by, 1926 was ending soon.

My freshly baked mandelbread, or what I once heard an Italian call them, biscotti, were cooling on the rack by the stove. They filled the kitchen with a wonderful smell. Freshly baked cookies, my favorite.

I poured my tea into a glass cup and drank it Russian style with lemon and sugar. No fancy schmancy milk in my tea like the Canadians drank.

Getting off my tired legs and swollen ankles was a pleasure. I had been busy all morning cooking for the delicatessen. Although the two eldest boys work full time and earn money I still needed the extra income I could earn to feed our growing family. I was pregnant again, child number six, or perhaps six and seven, it felt like I was having twins for a second time.

The smartest thing my husband ever did was move us to Toronto, away from Lithuania and the pogroms. Although life was tough and we barely had any money, we didn't have to worry about the Cossacks murdering us. We heard of a terrible pogrom in my former village where my poor sister and her family dug their own graves in the forest before they were shot. The longer we didn't receive a letter from them, the more in my heart I knew it must be true.

As tears rolled down my face I became angry at myself for using my precious peaceful time to think such sad thoughts. Wiping my tears away I thought about how I loved my children and how wonderful they were. They spoke the King's English with not a hint of a foreign accent to be heard. Real Canadians.

I took my first bite of the mandelbread.

Startled, I heard a knock on the door. I shouldn't have been surprised. I knew it was my next door neighbor Ethel who had some magical way of knowing the minute I had poured a fresh cup of tea and had baked cookies. She could beat the fastest race horse getting next door to my house.

"Leah Rivka, how are you?" She swept past me.

"Oh good, fresh tea and do I see your wonderful mandelbread? They smell as good as if they came from the Garden of Eden. Pour me a cup of tea, please."

I fixed her tea and put a nice plate of cookies on the table. She dug in right away.

"Leah Rivka, I don't know how you bake such wonderful cookies."

"Ethel, you know I bake for the deli, amongst the other things I make for them. I was up at 5:00 am making a large batch of kreplach for the deli. We need the money I earn to get by. The shoe repair business is slow."

"I've made cookies before, but they aren't as good as yours." Ethel gobbled up another mandelbread, thinking that a compliment made it okay for her to schnorr or scrounge my cookies all the time.

I sighed, "Ethel, the cookies you made and brought over when we moved here seven years ago were very good. You could make them even better if you practiced. In fact, if you ever made them a second time imagine how good they would be."

Ethel looked thoughtful and asked for more tea.

"Yes, Leah Rivka, that is a wonderful idea. I always think about baking again, but somehow I am drawn to your cookies, they are the best I ever had. I wouldn't want you to think that I was trying to be better than you."

Here was yet another compliment from the schnorrer trying to get out of work.

But she was my neighbor and my friend, I knew that as long as I lived next door I would always have a cup of tea and a treat ready for her.

We talked about Mrs. Jacob, who looked like she was pregnant with child number 10. How would she manage? Their house was even smaller than mine. The cost of food was going up all the time. How could any of us manage.

Suddenly the baby started to cry waking up from his nap.

"Sorry, Leah Rivka, I'd love to stay and help but I have to wash the kitchen floor. Bye!" she called out as she quickly escaped.

The little time sitting felt good and I slowly stood up to tend to the baby. Soon the older ones would be home from school and they would help me.

I grabbed another mandelbread and munched on it. I knew that Ethel would be back the moment I pulled out the next batch of cookies from the oven and the kettle was on.

# The Vacuum Cleaner Man

*Ruth Frankel-Graner*

You know what it's like. You hear a name, see a flash of something familiar, and it all comes roaring back.

When I was a young, and definitely naive housewife-a stay-at-home mom with three small children--cosily ensconced in the suburbs (make that trapped,) I had a vacuum cleaner man. No, I was not having an affair. He was old-at least thirty-five, but nicely dressed as most non-uniformed men I encountered in those days were. He wore a grey suit-perhaps a trifle worn-starched white shirt and an absolutely nondescript tie.

Perhaps that was a uniform, because way back when horses in Toronto delivered milk  (okay, pick yourself up off the floor, this isn't a ghost writing,   but a living, breathing ahem, senior,) well in those days, everyone from department store delivery men, to grocers, to those horse – wagon – driving milkmen – imagine that being part of the job description: "city deliveryman wanted, must be able to work with horses" – most working people up to and including behind the counter bakery, candy and even jewelry store clerks, wore uniforms of one kind or another. Unsurprisingly, I always wore an apron – I had quite a number of them – in my suburban V a l h a l l a.

Once a month –the first Wednesday of l believe, and usually in the afternoon – vacuum cleaner man (v.c.m.) made a house call. I know I didn't buy my vacuum cleaner from him, he just seemed to come with it. He would arrive on my doorstep, look me straight in the eye, "Just dropping by to check on that little beauty."

I would take her (?) out of the closet. He would gaze at my vacuum cleaner as though for the first time, stroke her handle and sigh, deeply. Then, with a knowing wink in my direction, as though we were co-conspirators, he'd smile, "Let's see if she's taking good care of you."

Of course I wasn't.

"Hmm, looks like she needs a bit of oil, Mrs. Frankel. Yesiree, oil a-plenty!"

I would cringe. I had failed vacuum cleaner school. He took a little squirt bottle out of his case, and applied the remedy, looking at me balefully, as if to say, "She's done it again!"

Of course that wasn't as bad as a worn belt.

"Why, that's just asking for trouble Mrs. Frankel. Begging for it! A bit more wear and I hate to think what might happen to that precious carpet of yours." That precious carpet was a remnant left over from my first apartment. It was the colour of a dead mouse, and wall- to-wall carpeting was the newest, latest thing. I hoped the belt would devour it, chew it to pieces. Then I would have to get wall-to-wall. But, as I said before, I was young and naive.

There was a zipper on the big vacuum cleaner bag, that held the little paper dust bags. My vacuum cleaner man would run this zipper up and down, tilting his head to listen to it, biting his lower lip. Tsk, tsking as though he wasn't quite satisfied, but what could you do?

The next potential source of vacuum cleaner catastrophe was the cord and plug. He would check them looking for G-d knows what, and if they passed the test-not easy, this man was a tough taskmaster-his next target was the small, disposable vacuum cleaner paper bags. I already had a cupboard full of them, but he had something newer, stronger, better. And, "What if I ran out of them and the Big Boss was coming for dinner?"

Well the Big Boss came for dinner every day. He was my husband. I was married to him!  "Sure, I'll take ten more bags, well make that twenty!"

I don't remember what each house call cost. I guess I could afford it. And perhaps it helped to feed the v.c.m.'s family. My kids moved out years ago, along with the Big Boss, and a green garbage bagful of aprons. I can't recall either when the vacuum cleaner man's visits stopped. Maybe when I moved away too, and neglected to give him my new address. I'm older now, and a little more worldly. If he reads this, I'm sure he'll forgive me.

# The Reluctant Shopper

*Sam Hoffer*

*Translated from the all-Yiddish CD, S'helft Nisht Keyn Krekhtsn! (There's No Use Complaining!) by Sam Hoffer.*

I don't know whether it's just us or in every family that everyone pokes his nose into everybody else's business.

Each Sunday, the whole gang, my brothers, their wives and their kids get together at our house. And, since my own kids and my nieces and nephews are all grown up, we're blessed not only with the mouth-watering foods that my wife so lovingly prepares but also with bountiful discussions about the latest political issues, all sorts of philosophical questions and always, our day-to-day troubles.

And so everything was going swimmingly last week until I happened to mention, with a sigh befitting my age, that I needed to buy myself a new pair of pants.

All at once, ten voices erupted. Each with an opinion about where I should buy the pants, who I should buy them from and what sort of fabric and style I should choose. Instantly, the room became a bazaar. And nobody cared a fig about what I thought.

After a few minutes they settled down and decided that whatever pants I bought, I had to get them at the Galaxy Shopping Center, from Schwartz's Fine Fabrics. And with that they left me alone.

As for me, I realized that if I wanted to avoid a battle the next time around, I'd simply have to go along.

And so, the day arrives and I set off for the Galaxy. A half-hour later, I see the sparkling rooftops of the massive stores in the distance. Wonderful. But as I get closer, I get the feeling that the entire city has converged here today to snap up the bargains. I drive around endlessly, looking for a parking spot and just when I find one, I see that there are already other cars waiting and that out of each window hangs an embittered face with crazed eyes threatening that if I even dream of taking the next parking spot, I should be prepared to die.

With God's help I find a spot. I crawl out of my car and begin to drag myself to the entrance to the shopping center. Finally I get there, look around and find a sea of stores. But no sign of Schwartz's.

There are hordes of people everywhere. They're trooping and lugging. Everyone loaded down with bags of stuff. I'm going nowhere. I'm frozen. Lost. But, all at once I notice a map on top of a large table surrounded by people. I inch closer and see that they are all bent over the table, with tortured looks on their faces. Whether they are actually searching for something or just trying to find the quickest way out of here is anybody's guess.

I squeeze through to the map and discover that Schwartz's is a mere five aisles to the left and three aisles up from where I am.

I'm schlepping yet again, until at last I get to my store. I barely enter, when I'm approached by a greeter. He confronts me with such a hearty "Welcome!" that you would think that I had single-handedly saved his life. I smile and no sooner do I return his greeting, then he forgets about me completely and rushes off to another customer.

I look around and see that I'm surrounded by an entire landscape of tables full of merchandise. Customers are gathered at the tables, checking out the goods. But there isn't a single salesperson in sight. So I ask one of the customers whether he knows where I might find a pair of pants. He gives me a look and tells me that if I follow the signs dangling from the ceiling, I'll find my way to the pants.

So now I'm searching the heavens and trudging once again.

According to the signs, there are all sorts of clothes here, but for the life of me I don't see any signs for pants. So I keep going until I do find – not pants, but shirts. Countless shirts. All styles, colours and sizes stretch as far as the eye can see. But no pants.

So once again I'm searching for a salesman. Forget it. But I notice a cash register on a table in the distance. I make my way there, figuring that just maybe a salesman will crawl out from under the table and help me. No such luck. But I see that there is a phone beside the cash register and a sign beside the phone. The sign says that if a customer has a problem, he should simply pick up the phone and someone will answer and help.

I pick up the phone and am greeted by a cheerful voice. I explain that I'm standing among the shirts but that I can't find any pants. The voice asks me why I'm standing among the shirts if what I want is pants. I reply that I don't actually need shirts but that I simply can't find the pants. So he says that since I'm among the shirts, it would be a shame if I didn't buy myself a shirt and then went hunting for pants.

I ask why it's so important to him that I should buy a shirt. He explains that he works for the shirt department and that it's his job to sell shirts, not pants. Pants, he says, are another operator's business. And how, I ask him, do I find the operator for the pants? He answers that I'll first have to find the pants and among the pants I'll find a phone and with that phone I'll be able to get in touch with the right operator. By now my head is spinning. I say nothing and hang up.

I look around and think. Since I can't find any pants, maybe I really should buy myself a nice shirt and just get out of here. I settle on a few shirts in various styles and colours. I step into the change room, try the shirts on and pick two. But, since I don't know my way around these things, I can't tell whether the shirts suit me or not.

So I'm again looking for a salesman, this time just to get an opinion. But it's a waste of time because it looks like absolutely nobody works here. I have no choice but to go back to the phone at the cash register. I pick up the phone and the same cheery voice greets me.

I tell the voice that I've picked two shirts but that I don't know whether they suit me or not. Without hesitating he says that he's sure that they are both excellent choices and that I should buy them both. I reply that I'm not your ordinary customer and that I'm surprised that he would offer an opinion without even seeing the shirts. He says I'm right and that if I want to be sure of my shirts, I should first match them up with my pants. And he asks, "have you managed to find your pants?"

My rage is overwhelming. "I HAVE NO PANTS!" I scream into the phone. "If I had pants I wouldn't need shirts! Don't mix me up! Make yourself crazy!"

I throw away the shirts and take off like a shot.

There are no salesmen! The phone is a waste of time! The greeter is running around like a chicken with his head cut off! There-is-no-one-to-talk-to!!!

*Note: Any resemblance in this story to real names and places is purely coincidental.*

# The Wedding

*Raizie Jacobson*

Berkley, California overlooking the Bay was the perfect setting for an outdoor wedding on a beautiful one-acre property. Stephanie and Jim chose the venue. They had been together for several years, and the bride spent much time planning the event and looking forward to a perfect day.

The guests were close family and friends who arrived from various locations in the U. S. to help Jim and Stephanie celebrate their union.

The wedding officiant was a rabbi of an unaffiliated congregation in the area. Though the groom was not Jewish, the couple tastefully blended Jewish traditions into the ceremony.

The guests sat on chairs neatly placed in rows on the grass looking out to the chuppah. They chattered amongst one another while waiting for the ceremony to begin. It was warm, and the groom pulled at his shirt collar, dabbed beads of perspiration on his forehead and smiled at the rabbi while they waited for the bride to arrive.

Stephanie prepared for her grand entrance. The music began playing and she beamed as she walked down the staircase, and when she reached the bottom, danced down the aisle towards Jim.

However, as Stephanie began her dance, one of her friends suddenly had a seizure and fell across the aisle, blocking Stephanie's approach. Everything stopped, and the guests hovered. Those who knew the woman were aware that she was subject to seizures, and were not alarmed by the incident. When the woman awoke, she was attended to by her friends who set her up in the shade under an umbrella which made her feel comfortable.

Now, Stephanie began again, proceeding down the stairs and continued dancing along the aisle towards the chuppah where Jim stood waiting. He turned and smiled at her, and the rabbi commenced the ceremony. The scene was tranquil as the hushed guests looked towards the smiling couple. Suddenly, in the midst of the solemnity of the occasion, a shrill scream pierced the silence from down the hill. "Someone is blocking my car!" a woman shrieked. With no response from the wedding guests, the ranting continued, her voice becoming louder. The guests looked at each other, but no one moved until the groom took matters into his own hands.

"Whoever has a vehicle blocking the woman's car, PLEASE move it immediately!" he said in a loud and slightly irritated voice. The culprits could longer ignore the irate woman or Jim. Two people hurried away, car keys in hand.

The screaming stopped and the unperturbed rabbi started the ceremony again. Everything went well until it was time to break the glass. The glass was placed on a tile so it would be easier to break than on the grass. Poor Jim stomped and stomped, but the glass wouldn't break. He gave it one more try, brought his foot down and shattered the tile; the glass however, remained intact. Jim said nothing, calmly picked up the glass, walked over to the concrete path, placed the glass on the ground, lifted his foot and smashed it. Mazel Tov!

I'm sure the guests will always remember Stephanie and Jim's wedding day as they celebrate many happy years together.

# Matching

*Carol Green*

I always loved to match my clothes. As far back as I can remember, I loved to coordinate the colours of my outfits. Apparently my Mother did the same thing when she was a child.

"Everything is matching with you," complained Grandpa to his young daughter.

He of the checked shirts with striped ties, worn with suspenders that connected the outfit together literally and chromatically. Grandpa dressed in the comfortable, slightly rumpled look of a country gentleman. The colours of his ensembles matched by chance. His look was at once, casual and formal. I liked it. When he went out, he added a fedora. But he did not match.

My own style has usually involved fastidious matching, even into recent history.

Until a few years ago, I owned a bright purple raincoat that I would wear with purple stockings. A purple umbrella completed the ensemble. When I wore this outfit, my husband called me "Barney" after the popular purple dinosaur on children's television. It did not change my zeal.

I remember in particular my adolescent fascination with bright shades. In my early teens, I loved orange and for a time had an orange "poorboy" sweater, orange fishnet stockings, orange Mary Jane shoes and orange jewellery. All worn with a school bus yellow skirt I had made out of canvas. This was even too much for my "matching" Mother. Maybe it was the orange – Mom detested orange.

I recall the lime-green cotton turtleneck worn with lime-green knee socks and a matching hair ribbon that I wore during high school. I came upon the hair ribbon in my things the other day – I remembered how hard it was to find just the right shade of velvet ribbon – two bus rides to downtown Ottawa fabric stores. My friends were impressed. "Carol always matches," they said. My friend, Jeanette, often asked me to describe the colours I wore: "candy apple red, lemon yellow, dusky rose, pale cream"…Jeanette loved the sounds of my descriptions.

I can't say why I loved matching. I care less about it now, although I still mostly match when I go out in the morning. And I notice when other individual's garments don't match, although I try not to be judgmental about it. Once a matcher, always a matcher. Indeed, a fellow member of my writing group, who was also a "matcher," was impressed with my flair for coordinating my clothes. We used to regularly conduct "matching checks" on each other.

In middle age, I do not even know what is fashionable anymore. The other day, a teenage girl down the street told me my shoes and purse were "hot." I didn't tell her that the reason I bought the shoes was because they were comfortable. And the bag was large enough to carry all my stuff. But they did match.

# A Tribute to Earth Hour

*Sam Hoffer*

*Earth Hour is an annual call to people around the world to acknowledge, through a small but meaningful act, the sanctity of our Earth. This tribute was presented by Sam Hoffer at the Beth Tzedec Synagogue, in Toronto, to commemorate Earth Hour in March of 2012.*

It is not entirely well known that in the early 1900's, some Jewish farming colonies were established on the Canadian prairies. One of these was the Sonnenfeld Colony in the midst of which was a tiny hamlet named after its founders, Mayer and Israel Hoffer, distant relatives of mine. In its earliest years, this colony, like other frontier Jewish settlements, offered young Jewish men and women the opportunity to become masters of their own fate in Canada, in ways that they simply could not have done in the countries of their origin in Eastern Europe.

A second set of immigrants arrived in the colony immediately after the Second World War. My parents and my two older brothers, survivors of Transnistria and I, born right after the war, were among these more recent arrivals. Altogether, we were a community of some twenty Jewish families.

Although the challenges facing pioneers in the early 1900's can only be imagined, life for us, even 50 years later, was harsh. We lived in a farmhouse made of wood boards, with no furnace to battle the 40-below-zero temperatures, no electricity, no telephone and no indoor plumbing. We got our drinking water from a well at the bottom of the hill that our house stood on, a feat that involved carrying each pail uphill over snowdrifts in the bitter cold and biting wind.

But nature rewarded us with untold beauty as well. The rooster crowing at each break of dawn; the bright, blinding sun in the still of the morning; the gentle breeze that gathered the scent of budding crops and enveloped us in a cocoon of comfort and promise; the crimson sunsets; the milky way that glistened across a boundless sky; the majestic northern lights that draped us in a curtain of rainbows in the night. These were all miracles of nature.

There were other treats too for a young and fascinated mind. Watching my father milk the cow and scooping a drink right out of the milk pail; seeing him gather the cream and tirelessly stir it with a wooden spoon until it turned to butter; studying his every move as he carefully hollowed out raw potatoes, filling the cavities with oil and fashioning our own miracle of Chanukah.

And my mother braiding challahs on Friday morning, coating them lovingly with a chicken feather dipped in egg, her outstretched hands gathering the light of the Shabbos candles and blessing them in a house dimly lit by coal oil lamps but bright with affection and gratitude.

Still other things characterised life in our small Jewish community.

Occasional gatherings at our house where the favourite contest among the men was a card game called whist; where my father entertained the others who were more inclined to listen to him read stories from the Yiddish newspaper that came to us all the way from New York; where the anticipated refreshment was "vursht" sandwiches made of rye bread and salami imported all the way from Winnipeg.

Then there were the High Holidays, when my father walked the country roads for miles to our skeletal synagogue in Hoffer and somehow found the strength to lead the prayers.

And there was The Jewish Hour that we listened to on the car radio every Sunday morning, our window to the Jewish world.

And Yiddish, spoken by everyone, freely, fluently, in sorrow and in joy. A language that we had not yet lost.

These, as much as the wonders of nature, were the roots that nourished and shaped us.

Earth Hour is a precious idea. It is a reminder of the importance of being mindful and deliberate so that we will treasure all that makes us who we are, in nature and in life.

# Acknowledgements

There are a number of people who in various capacities helped launch A Cup of Roses, Stories by 8 Writers. Thank you to Lenore Villeneuve, Ruth Frankel-Graner's daughter who graciously approved the publication of Ruth's stories, Greg Ioannou, Meghan Behse, Dr. Robert Kroll, Rabbi Jarrod Grover and Doris Alter.

The Anthology was the brainchild and a dream of Ruth Frankel-Graner. Fiona Gold Kroll took this dream and through hard work and perseverance turned it into reality. Thank you to Jenny Roger and Sam Hoffer, who became Fiona's sounding board throughout the process.

Finally, thank you to the individual authors who contributed their work: the late Ruth Frankel-Graner, Gerda Frieberg, Carol Green, Sam Hoffer, Raizie Jacobson, Fiona Gold Kroll, Dr David Rapoport and Jenny Roger.

# Biographies

**Ruth Frankel-Graner** was an inspired artist and writer who lived in Toronto. She taught English north of the city before she retired. She formed and led the writers group at Beth Tikvah Synagogue. Ruth had several short stories published, two in the Toronto Globe & Mail, and two more in the Canadian Jewish News. She was in the process of putting together her Book of Miracles before her untimely passing in 2015.

**Gerda Frieberg** is a Holocaust survivor. After making her home in Toronto she made Holocaust education her priority. She has served as president and chaired numerous committees in Canada and is the recipient of several achievement awards. Gerda is a retired business woman who also learned to fly a plane and became the first female instrument rated pilot in Toronto. In 2013, Gerda published her memoirs I kept My Promise followed by her second book Never A Bystander.

**Carol Green** is a native of Ottawa. Carol wrote social welfare publications for government and the non-profit sector in London, Ont., before moving to Toronto. She was a frequent columnist for the community newspaper of Fairlawn Avenue United Church, distributed to 5,000+ households. She also contributed to two anthologies of The Canadian Poetry Institute (Hot Flash Breakfast and Unwanted Hair), and recently completed her autobiography Laughing All the Way. Carol lives in Thornhill with her family and continues to write short stories filled with nostalgia, family and humour.

**Sam Hoffer** writes short stories and poetry and is completing a memoir of his childhood on the prairies, *An Uncertain Dawn*, excerpts from which have been published in the Canadian Jewish News. He has released a CD of original Yiddish tales entitled, *S'helft nisht keyn krekhtsn!* (*There's No Use Complaining!*) selections of which were broadcast on Yiddish Forward Radio, New York (www.yiddishstories.com). His short story, *A Portrait in Time*, was published in the September, 2016 issue of Jewish Fiction.net (www.jewishfiction.net). Hoffer is also active in the visual arts as a photographer and producer of video biographies.

**Raizie Jacobson** is formerly from Winnipeg and has been writing for fun since grade school where she won many awards for her stories. Until recently, Raizie led the book club at Beth Tikvah synagogue in Toronto. Today, she applies the skills she used as a former telecom analyst to observe and record the quirks and challenges of everyday life. This is her first published work.

**Fiona Gold Kroll** is the author of A Stone for Benjamin, by Iguana Books. Fiona has appeared on Rogers TV and continues to speak with various groups about her quest to discover her great-uncle's fate. She has published several short stories, including The Butterfly Effect, in The Globe & Mail and When a Daughter Leaves the Shtetl, and Shabbat Shalom both published in The Canadian Jewish News. You can follow her on social media and at www.fionagoldkroll.com. Fiona lives in Toronto with her family and continues to write short stories, novellas and novels.

**Dr. David Rapoport** is a recently retired family physician. For more than 20 years, David has been writing about the lighter side of medicine in Family Practice and Medical Post magazines. They both devoted their last page to medical humour, with an illustrated story. In 2015 David wrote and published "It all begins in the waiting room..." This book brings together seventy of the popular stories David wrote for the magazines. David continues to write in Toronto, where he lives with his family.

**Jenny Roger** is a former preschool instructor who morphed into a Toronto Food Blogger and is an Inspirational Gastroposter having many food photos published in the National Post, Gastropost Section. Feeding Family and Friends. You can find Jenny @icecreamandknishes.com

# Sources


"Heading South? Eater Beware: or How I Saved an Entire Country from Disaster" by Ruth Frankel-Graner © 2015 First published in *The Globe and Mail*, April 27, 2015. Reprinted by permission of the author's estate.

"Broken Dreams" by Gerda Frieberg © 2016.

"How I Became a Jewish Writer" by Carol Green © 2016.

"Day One" by Sam Hoffer © 2016.

"Ben's War" by Fiona Gold Kroll © 2016.

"Too Close for Comfort" by Raizie Jacobson © 2016.

"The Ancient Synagogue of Barcelona" by Jenny Roger © 2016.

"Mother knows best: enlisting her as a waiting room spy" by David Rapoport © 2015. First published in "It All Begins in the Waiting Room: How to drive your doctor crazy while escaping retaliation" © by David Rapoport, 2015. Reprinted by permission of the author.

"First Flower" by Sam Hoffer © 2016.

"Blue Plaid" by Ruth Frankel-Graner © 2016.

"Flying Solo" by Gerda Frieberg © Adapted from "I Kept My Promise" © by Gerda Frieberg, 2013. Reprinted by permission of the author.

"Poppies" by Fiona Gold Kroll © 2016.

"The World's Oldest Food Blogger" by Jenny Roger © 2016.

"The Winner" by Carol Green © 2016.

"Gentle Paces" by Sam Hoffer © 2016.

"Two Petals Lost" by Carol Green © 2016.

"Vilna Vegetarian" by Jenny Roger © 2016.

"SPINACH WRAP at The True Blue Wooden House Restaurant" by Ruth Frankel-Graner © 2016.

"The Mezuzah" by Fiona Gold Kroll © 2016.

"A Boundless Journey" by Sam Hoffer © 2016.

"Still A Prisoner" by Gerda Frieberg © 2016.

"Matzo Balls" by Jenny Roger © 2016.

"Paris City of Lights" by Raizie Jacobson © 2016.

"How Did This Dog Happen?" by Sam Hoffer © First published in *Havanese Breed Magazine*, May/June 2015. Reprinted by permission of the author.

"Hotel Fire" by Carol Green © 2016.

"When a Daughter Leaves the Shtetl" by Fiona Gold Kroll © 2015 First published in *The Canadian Jewish News*, April 2015. Reprinted by permission of the author.

"Our Picture" by Carol Green © 2016.

"Burned Money" By Gerda Frieberg © Adapted from "I Kept My Promise" © by Gerda Frieberg, 2013. Reprinted by permission of the author.

"The Kettle" by Jenny Roger © 2016.

"The Vacuum Cleaner Man" by Ruth Frankel-Graner © 2016.

"The Reluctant Shopper" by Sam Hoffer © 2009 Translated from the all- Yiddish CD, S'helft Nisht Keyn Krekhtsn! (There's No Use Complaining!) by Sam Hoffer 2009. Printed by permission of the author.

"The Wedding" by Raizie Jacobson © 2016.

"Matching" by Carol Green © 2016.

"Earth Hour" by Sam Hoffer © 2012 Presented at Beth Tzedec Synagogue to commemorate Earth Hour March 2012. Printed by permission of the author.

www.ingramcontent.com/pod-product-compliance
Lightning Source LLC
Chambersburg PA
CBHW021022120726
47905CB00009B/3140